Ffordd y Bannau
The Beacons Way

Holy Mountain to Bethlehem

'At some period, the night of the Crucifixion, say the locals, and call it in consequence "The Holy Mountain", a great landslip clave its summit in half, leaving one side precipitous...'

A.G. Bradley

Ffordd y Bannau
The Beacons Way

Holy Mountain to Bethlehem

The Official Trail of The Brecon Beacons
National Park Authority

Text: John Sansom & Arwel Michael

Photographs: Chris Barber

First published in 2005 by Walking Wales Magazine Ltd.

This edition published by Blorenge Books, Blorenge Cottage,
Church Lane, Llanfoist, Abergavenny NP7 9NG.
Telephone 01873 856114

ISBN 1 872730 44 2

Text © John Sansom & Arwel Michael 2005

Revision of route in 2010 by Chris Barber,
Robert Knowles and Kirsty Mallindine

Photography © Chris Barber MBE FRGS

Front cover photograph: Below Waun Lefrith, Carmarthen Fans
Back cover photograph: Pen y Fan, Brecon Beacons

All rights reserved. This publication must not be reproduced in
any form without prior permission from the publisher.

Whilst every effort has been made to ensure that the information
in this book is correct the authors or publisher can accept no
responsibility for errors, loss or injury however caused.

Map extracts reproduced by permission of Ordnance Survey on
behlaf of HMSO © Crown Copyright 2011. All rights reserved.
OS Licence number: 100051334

Printed by MWL Print Group Ltd. Tel: 01495 750033

CONTENTS

Introduction

IT was during the dark days of the foot and mouth disease outbreak in 2001 that this trail took shape. Throughout that period access to the pastures and uplands of the Brecon Beacons National Park was, for the most part, totally forbidden for over six months. The impact that this closure had on tourism was considerable and the value of tourism to the rural economy became starkly apparent.

Whilst foot and mouth restrictions were at their height the Brecon Beacons National Park Authority set up three working parties to look at the future for the National Park when the countryside reopened. Since the impact of the disease on tourism had been so great one of these working parties looked at what could be done to restore, not just the status quo, but to consider what further boosts were needed to revive tourism in the area. The truth was that, even before the outbreak of foot and mouth, visitor numbers had been in decline for a variety of complex reasons.

The Brecon Beacons Park Society was represented on these working parties. It was whilst a member of the tourism working party was telling the Executive Committee of the Society about the proceedings of the Tourism Working Party that the idea of a Beacons Trail was born. Most National Parks have specially dedicated trails, way marked and promoted by a guide book giving information about the archaeology, history, geology and folklore of the area. The Brecon Beacons National Park had no such route. The Offa's Dyke National Trail goes along part of its eastern perimeter: the Taff Trail from Cardiff to Brecon uses two routes across the central Beacons: the Usk Valley Walk starting near Newport follows the Vale of Usk into the National Park. The Cambrian Way, a north-south Wales route still awaiting official recognition, gives walkers the most comprehensive view of the Park but with such a large remit and such a lot of ground to cover, it does not specifically explore the special features of the Brecon Beacons National Park.

The popularity of these trails is well attested. Those with 'National' status receive special funding. Such trails are hard to set up and it was clear that to go for national status would extend the period of gestation and probably be beyond the ability of the Park Society to promote.

The Brecon Beacons National Park Authority has done a very good job opening up the rights of way within its boundaries. Furthermore most of the upland areas of the National Park are common land over which there are rights to roam. The high level of access already enjoyed would make the task of creating a trans-park trail much easier.

In the event, the process of getting the trail together took longer than intended. It is very much the work of two individuals. They apologise now for any misinformation or unclear guidance they have given. They also hope that they have properly acknowledged all sources of information.

Throughout the enterprise the National Park Authority has been very supportive and upon them has fallen the task of providing the waymarking to aid walkers in their passage across the farmland paths. The routes on the open hills and across commons are not waymarked. Such intrusive signing has never been the Authority's policy.

Credit must also go to Chris Barber who has drawn on his collection of photographs, built up over 40 years, to illustrate this guide. He too has offered the project great support in so many ways and we are deeply indebted to him.

The Trail goes into two National Nature Reserves and the Countryside Council for Wales has encouraged our use of these two sites. We have consulted the National Trust which owns the Skirrid and a large amount of the Central Beacons which we cross during the walk. They too have supported the project.

The Brecon Beacons National Park

The Brecon Beacons National Park was created in 1957. It is one of a family of National Parks throughout the U.K. and one of three in Wales. It covers land in what was then known as Monmouthshire (59 square miles), Breconshire (344 square miles), Carmarthenshire (87 square miles) and Glamorgan (29 square miles). Since its formation new 'Unitary Authorities' have been created and then extinguished and recreated under new names with different boundaries. At the current count the National Park's boundaries extend into nine different authorities and who knows what the future will bring.

The formation of the Brecon Beacons National Park brought together areas which had, and still have today, distinct identities. The Brecon Beacons National Park is very much an artificial construction.

Before the creation of the Lake District and the Peak District National Parks, to mention but two, residents of those areas would have recognised that they were living in the Lake District or the Peak District. This was not the case in the Brecon Beacons National Park. Here residents and visitors are more likely to think of the Park, not in its entirety but in terms of its constituent parts. Llanthony residents will see themselves as living in the Monmouthshire Black Mountains. In the west of the Park, the reference point is Mynydd Du, also known as the Black Mountain or the Carmarthen Fans.

Visitors to the Llanthony Valley are surprised and puzzled to find that it is in the 'Brecon Beacons' or the 'Beacons' as it is sometimes called. News items describe events as happening in the Brecon Beacons when they really mean that it has taken place within the territory over which the Brecon Beacons National Park Authority exercises certain powers.

The powers exercised by all the Welsh National Park Authorities are in the process of being reviewed. At present there are two primary statutory functions:

1. To conserve and enhance the natural beauty, wildlife and cultural heritage of the Park.
2. To promote the understanding and enjoyment of the special qualities of the National Park.

There is a third purpose which they should also attempt to achieve 'without incurring significant expenditure' which is to foster economic and social wellbeing within the Park.

The Beacons Way, which has the full support of the National Park Authority, is very much a manifestation of the second statutory function of promoting understanding and enjoyment of the special features of this beautiful landscape.

So let us look at what the Brecon Beacons National Park is all about.

The Naming of the Parts

Those of us who have known the area for a long time still think of the easterly upland block of the National Park as the Monmouthshire Black Mountains (although most of the area is in Breconshire and a small part in Herefordshire). The central part of the Park was always referred to as the Brecon Beacons and the westerly uplands were known as the Carmarthen Fans (although the highest point was in Breconshire). It is now politically correct to refer to the Monmouthshire Black Mountains simply as the Black Mountains. The Carmarthen Fans are now known as the Black Mountain or Mynydd Du. Between the Brecon Beacons and the Black Mountain (Carmarthen Fans) another area is distinguished. This is Fforest Fawr (The Great Forest), an ancient royal hunting ground. In the middle ages its 40,000 acres would have been more wooded than now. The present area defined as Fforest Fawr is less extensive than the royal forest of the middle ages.

The most natural of all features links these four areas: it is their geology. As you make your way about the Park it is the geology, and Man's often puny impact on it, that most effects what you see and experience.

Geology and Scenery

Old Red Sandstone
The highest peaks are all of Old Red Sandstone. From Hay Bluff in the east to Bannau Sir Gaer in the west there is a series of high hills and mountains, some with north or northwest facing massive escarpments, which give the National Park its distinctive skylines. Indeed, it is this feature which pulls together the differing sections of the National Park.

Brecon Beacons from the A40 at Llanhamlach

Although these uplands have much in common, the ridges and valleys that lie to the south of the scarps are markedly different and contribute to the Park's considerable scenic variety.

For example, in the Brecon Beacons a number of the valleys have been flooded for reservoirs and there is extensive forestry. In the Black Mountains, only one of the four large valleys has a reservoir and in that valley only is there extensive forestry. Farming is the predominant use of the Black Mountains valleys and foothills. In the Black Mountain (Carmarthen Fans) the country immediately south of the escarpment consists of carboniferous deposits giving rise to an entirely different landscape. To the north is one reservoir and some forestry and farms extending to the northern boundary of the Park.

Old Red Sandstone deposits were quarried in the past mainly for building stone and roof tiles. The use of sandstone for roof tiles is a feature of the regions vernacular architecture. Reservoir construction made use of local stone. Old Red Sandstone quarrying has been on a relatively small scale. Its impact on the scenery has not been great and often provides an interesting feature in the landscape as well as creating the opportunity for greater biodiversity.

The sandstone deposits sometimes contain a calcareous band of stone which, when streams drain through it, give rise to a deposit known as tufa. The presence of the lime rich deposits has an interesting effect on the flora as has the alkaline waters of the springs. It causes acid soil preferring plants to grow in close association with lime lovers. Sometimes these calcareous bands have been quarried as at Henallt Common 2.5km south of Hay. The workings are visible on the southern boundary of the common and a ruined kiln exists at the western end of the deposit.

North west of Capel-y-ffin, at the base of Tarren yr Esgob cliffs, there is a curious lump of rock known locally as the Honeycomb Rock. It has fallen from the cliffs above where more of it can be seen. The remains of a recently discovered small limekiln nearby shows that these deposits, like those at Henallt, were converted into agricultural lime for local use.

Carboniferous Limestone, Milstone Grit and the Lower Coal Measures

Along the southern fringe of the National Park, the Old Red Sandstone is overlain by Limestone deposits which vary in thickness and extent and which are in turn overlain by Millstone Grit.

The characteristic feature of this landscape is the pock marked, cratered moorland caused by the collapse of cave systems lying underneath the millstone grit. These sink holes (also known as swallow holes or shake holes) extend right across the Park's southern perimeter. In no other part of Britain are so many sinkholes to be found.

Porth yr Ogof has the largest cave entrance in Wales

Cave systems abound. Over the millennia streams have cut their way though the rocks forming spectacular gorges such as the Clydach Gorge to the east of the Park and splendid waterfalls on the rivers Nedd, Mellte and Hepste.

Limestone has been quarried over the centuries for building, industrial, civil engineering and agricultural purposes. The scars of the old and the new quarries are very much a feature of the southern fringe. Many limestone quarries have ceased operation in recent years and some provide suitable sites for developing climbing skills. The quarrying has sometimes provided cavers with new access to the cave systems.

The major caving sites are at:

Pwll du: at the head of Cwm Llanwenarth 2.5km (1.5 miles) north of Blaenavon. This is the most recently discovered system and may prove to be the largest in the British Isles. **Llangattock Escarpment**: Agen Alwedd and Darren Cilau. **Tawe Valley**: Ogof Ffynnon Ddu and Dan yr Ogof Show caves.

In the far west of the Park the carboniferous deposits were much exploited over the years to service the iron and steel industries of the Swansea Valley in particular.

The Lower Coal Measures make an appearance along the southern fringe of the Park and despite much clearing up of slag heaps they are not a pretty site. Recently open cast mining has impinged on the Park's southern boundary. An attempt to create a vast opencast mine just above the Clydach Gorge was fought off after a very long Public Inquiry. One area, just north of Blaenavon, has achieved the status of a World Heritage Site because of the importance of its industrial archaeology. Great things are planned for this area of industrial dereliction. In the west of the Park, between Ystradgynlais and Brynamman, local people are exerting pressure to restore their ravaged landscape and hold back further exploitation.

Big Pit National Mining Museum, Blaenavon World Heritage Site

The Ice Age

During the Ice Age the mountains of the National Park generated glaciers and ice sheets which shaped the landscape within and outside the Park. The glaciers formed the cwms (or corries) that lie at the foot of some of the scarps. The little lakes of Llyn y Fan Fach and Llyn y Fan Fawr in the Black Mountain and Llyn Cwm Llwch below Corn Du and Pen y Fan in the Brecon Beacons are notable examples. There are many more such hollows. Most do not feature lakes although they may well be very waterlogged and below the Llangattock escarpment have given rise to a raised bog. Somewhat grander is Llangorse Lake, formed by a gigantic glacial scoop.

Llyn Cwm Llwch in the Brecon Beacons

Moraines, great piles of glacial debris, are a common feature of the landscape. One such moraine managed to divert the course of the River Honddu at the end of the Llanthony Valley and to divert the River Monnow. It blocked their original course to the River Usk at Abergavenny causing them to flow north, join up and end as a tributary of the Wye.

The Post Glacial Period

Peat formation and degradation
The most important post glacial change to widely effect the landscape of the National Park has been the formation of peat deposits on the hills. These deposits have built up over the last 5000 years and support heather moors and grazing. Anyone familiar with the upland areas will know that in many places these peat deposits are eroding away and exposing the rock and thin mineral soils beneath. The causes of this erosion are many and varied but man has certainly played a role in assisting it in some locations. Not only is the heather moorland under threat; the grasslands are also endangered.

Landslides

There are a number of examples of landslides but the two most spectacular are those in the Black Mountains at Cwmyoy and on the Skirrid Mountain (Ysgyryd Fawr – The Holy Mountain). The one at Cwmyoy has an added interest.

Cwmyoy Church in the Llanthony Valley

The ancient church (12th Century) was built on unstable land associated with the landslide. Over the ensuing centuries the church buckled and writhed as the land moved beneath it. Miraculously, it has not fallen down yet! Its tower is said to lean more than the Tower of Pisa. Buttresses, stays and braces have been put in place to keep the tottering edifice from falling over.

Finally, the oldest rocks that appear in the Park must not be forgotten.

Silurian and Ordovician

Along what can best be described as the Park's northwestern boundary, the oldest rocks in the Park make an appearance. The ridge of Trichrug, southeast of Bethlehem, is formed from rocks of the Silurian series which are typically shales and fossil bearing sandstones.

Although the National Park is more than its rocks, they, more than any thing else, shape the landscape, and support or challenge man's presence in it.

The Prehistoric Landscape

Following the retreat of the glaciers the first identifiable settlers moved into the area covered by the National Park. Just south of the National Park, at Paviland Cave on Gower, evidence of occupation during the Ice Age was discovered but no such sites have been found in the Park.

The Mesolithic Age 7500BC–4500BC

The first identifiable settlers left no monuments and the evidence that exists of their presence is mainly confined to worked flint tools. Waun Fignan Felin, the peat bog to the southwest of Fan Hir on the Black Mountain, has produced a quantity of flint and analysis of the peat deposits has shown that clearing of the vegetation took place around this site which at that time (about 7500 to 5500 BC) was a lake.

The Neolithic Age 4500BC–2000BC

The first structural remains we see in the Park belong to that part of the period which extended from 3500 to 2000BC. A number of these monuments are still very impressive. Perhaps the most notable is the chambered tomb at Penywyrlod (approx 2.2 km south of Talgarth). This was discovered in 1972 when the quarrying of a large mound revealed human skeletal remains and a subsequent limited excavation confirmed seventeen burials. The tomb is 55 metres long and 25 metres at its widest part. It would have stood 3 metres high. The tomb is in the care of CADW which is the Welsh equivalent of English Heritage. It can be approached by a footpath but at the time of writing there is no on site interpretation.

A number of chambered tombs of this period are to be found in the Park but none lie on the route taken by the Beacons Way.

Standing stones, stone circles and stone alignments are associated with the latter end of the Neolithic and are also to be found associated with monuments of an Early Bronze Age dating.

The Bronze Age 2000BC–800BC

Whilst the Beacons Way does not go near any of the chambered tombs it literally makes contact with many of the monuments of the Late Neolithic and Early Bronze Age.

This particular prehistoric period did much to shape the upland landscape we now enjoy. This period enjoyed a warm, dry climate. Warmer in fact than we are experiencing today. Then the uplands

uplands were extensive areas of grassland and scrub providing good opportunities for hunting. Some areas, now open hill, were under cultivation. When the climate grew cooler and wetter the peat which covers these uplands began to form, perhaps aided by overcultivation and overstocking.

The use of the uplands for hunting is well proven in the Black Mountains where good examples of arrowheads and scrapers for dressing and cutting skins are frequently found. The Offa's Dyke footpath yields many such finds, washed out of the peat deposits to either side of the track during heavy rain. If you stumble across any please note the location and donate it to Abergavenny Museum.

The most obvious monuments of the Bronze Age are the numerous round cairns, of all shapes and sizes, that crown many of the summits and ridges of the mountains and moorlands of the National Park. Whereas the chambered tombs were used for multiple burials, the round cairns of the Bronze Age were sometimes the graves of an individual who was probably a prominent member of their society. Other round cairns show signs of several burials taking place over a period of time. Most of these cairns were opened up by treasure hunters in times gone by and much material relating to them has been lost.

In addition, a number of circular enclosures and field enclosure systems may date from this period.
It could be that the upland areas of the National Park were more extensively populated during this period than at any time before or since.

The Iron Age 800 BC–50 AD
The Iron Age is well represented in the National Park. Along the Usk Valley, on both its flanks, and on the high points above tributary streams such as the Clydach and Rhiangol there are many hill forts and enclosures of Iron Age date.

On the first leg of the Beacons Way two such forts are evident. The first on the summit of Holy Mountain, the Skirrid, which is a relatively obscure earth work and the second is the Pentwyn Hill Fort at the beginning of the walk along Hatterrall Hill. This fort is particularly large and its northern ramparts are clearly visible from the Hereford - Abergavenny road.

On the second day the Beacons Way takes you to the impressive fort on Table Mountain above Crickhowell. Here it is just about possible to pick out the circular foundations of huts that existed in the fort's interior.

Garn Goch is one of the largest Iron Age hill forts in Wales

On the final day of the trail, close to the hamlet of Bethlehem, you will walk through the largest hill fort in Wales at Garn Goch. Only a few paces from this fort (Y Gaer fawr) lies a smaller one called (Y Gaer fach) which is believed to have been built at the same date. This is described in some detail in the text.

The hill forts usually consist of one or two defensive deep ditches of rectangular or circular shape. Some sites have more than one enclosure and were clearly enlarged after the initial construction. The wall on top of the ditch could be of stone and/or a wooden stockade. The entrance was built in such a way as to deter invaders. These invaders would probably have been from neighbouring clans.

Most hillforts have no supply of water within them. They could not therefore withstand a siege. Many contain hut circles and were occupied all the time and may well have contained workshops of various sorts. Some of these hillforts are of a very grand design and one is led to conclude that they may have been early examples of conspicuous consumption aimed at impressing neighbours.

Tighten the muscle, feel the strong blood flow, and set your foot upon the utmost crest!'

Geoffrey Winthrop Young

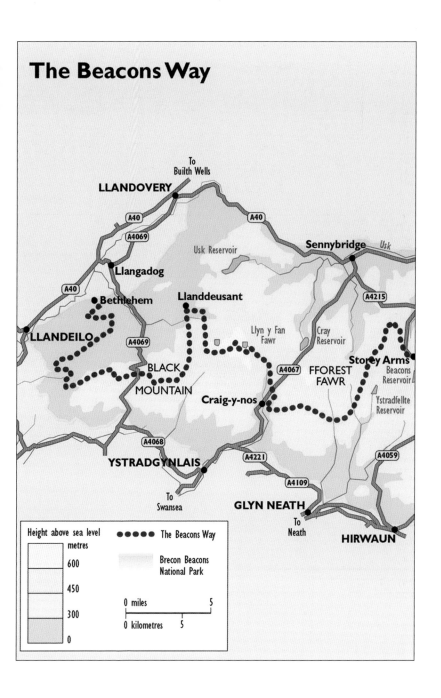

The Beacons Way

To Builth Wells

LLANDOVERY

A40

A40

A4069

Usk Reservoir

Sennybridge *Usk*

Llangadog

A40

A4215

Bethlehem

Llanddeusant

LLANDEILO

A4069

Llyn y Fan Fawr

Cray Reservoir

Storey Arms

Beacons Reservoir

BLACK

A4067

FFOREST FAWR

MOUNTAIN

Ystradfellte Reservoir

Craig-y-nos

A4068

A4221

A4059

YSTRADGYNLAIS

A4109

To Swansea

GLYN NEATH

To Neath

HIRWAUN

Height above sea level
metres

●●●●● The Beacons Way

Brecon Beacons National Park

600

0 miles   5

450

0 kilometres   5

300

0

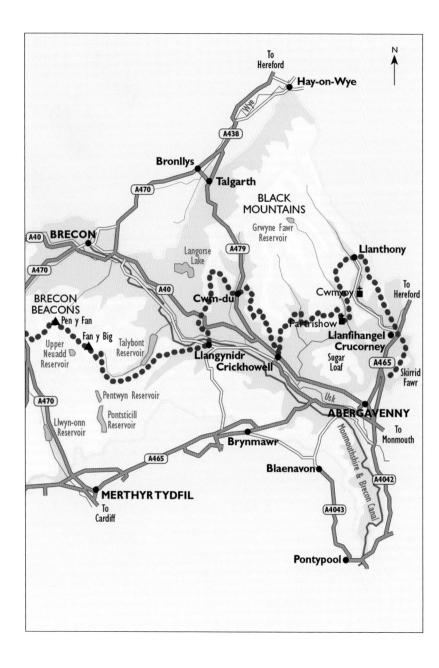

THE ROUTE: *An overview*

THE route of the Beacons Way is designed to present this beautiful part of Wales in the very best possible light. It is an area of high hills, deep valleys and expansive moorland. Traversing it will involve a lot of climbing and the crossing of some very exposed upland. The route will not be waymarked over open hills and commons.

Good route navigational skills are essential. Since the route goes into the hills bad weather can have a very serious effect on the conditions. No person inexperienced in hill walking, should attempt this trail unless accompanied by an experienced guide.

The trail sometimes goes off the beaten track taking routes not usually explored by the average walker. The route is, for the most part, not too rough underfoot. It is neither an endurance test nor a mountain challenge event. It is within the competence of any fit rambler or walker accustomed to energetic hill walking. It is more demanding than walking in Exmoor, Dartmoor, the North York Moors, the Peak District and the Yorkshire Dales. It is not as challenging as Snowdonia, the Lake District or many parts of Scotland. When a section of the trail is particularly tough the following day's trek will be less demanding.

The route is described in some detail but the maps in the text will tell the walker more than words ever can.

Walkers will need the Brecon Beacons National Park 1:25,000 Ordnance Survey maps to enable them to see the trail in its full context. Without these maps, in bad weather or emergencies, it will be impossible to devise escape routes.

In the far west, on the final day of the walk, the current edition of the Central and Western National Park map omits a small section of the Park and the Beacons Way just finds its way off the map before swinging round onto it again. The map in the text will totally meet the needs of the walker.

The ability to read a map and use a compass is essential. The best of days can turn nasty and even on a good day the summits may be swathed in mist.

The most physically demanding section of the trail is on the fourth day from Llangynidr to Storey Arms. The route from Craig Cerrig-gleisiad to Craig-y-nôs is tricky in thick fog. Craig-y-nôs to Llanddeusant is inadvisable in bad weather. Whereas the route from Llanddeusant Youth Hostel to Carreg Cennen castle is difficult in foggy conditions.

Two Youth Hostels are on and close to the route. Both close during the winter months and are often fully booked, thus advance booking is essential.

Note: From time to time footpaths are legally diverted and new permitted paths are created. When this happens on the Beacons Way the resulting new route will be signed and waymarked.

DAY	ROUTE	MILES	KM	ASCENT FEET	ASCENT METRES
1	Holy Mountain to Llanthony	10.6	17	2270	697
2	Llanthony to Crickhowell	12	19.5	3063	934
3	Crickhowell to Llangynidr	12.2	19.5	2230	680
4	Llangynifr to Storey Arms	14.2	22.7	3345	1020
5	Storey Arms to Craig-y-nos	14.75	23.7	1820	555
6	Craig-y-nos to Llanddeusant	10.5	16.8	2558	780
7	Llanddeusant to Carreg Cennen	13.6	21.8	2591	790
8	Carreg Cennen to Bethlehem	6.8	10.9	787	240
	TOTALS	94.6	151.7	18682	5696

Note: The maps included in this guidebook are extracts from the OS Landranger series, scale 1:50000 and they are meant solely as a guide. To walk the route safely one should be equipped with OS Explorer maps (OL12 and OL13), scale 1: 25000.

'Maps are always a treasured possession of the mountaineer. They are the charts by which he steers his course, and above all, perhaps, they serve to recall his memories of great days spent among the hills. Maps are essential to a full enjoyment of his sport and under some conditions may be essential to his safety.'

G.A. Lister 1924

Ffordd y Bannau
The Beacons Way
The Holy Mountain to Bethlehem

DAY ONE
Holy Mountain to Llanthony

Distance: Skirrid car park 10.6 miles/17km
Ascent: 2270 feet/697m   Map: Explorer 13

Start from the Skirrid Car Park
The route from the car park to the summit is easy to follow along an obvious ever-ascending track.

From the car park take the track up between the two planted hedgerows. Not so long ago this was a much narrower track. The National Trust widened it and put in the hedging. At the head of this track a gate leads into the wood. Take the path straight ahead of you that goes onwards and upwards until you come to another gate that leads onto the hill. Go through that gate and turn right following the well worn and, for part of its way, stone pitched path that heads up through scrubby woodland to the bare hill. Then just press on for the next kilometre (1100 yards) until you reach the summit.

'Take nothing but photographs: kill nothing but time. Leave nothing but your bootprints and goodwill.'

© Crown Copyright 2011. All rights reserved. OS Licence number: 100051334

William Coxe made his way to the summit in 1799 and this is how he felt.....

'....the effort I impatiently made to reach the summit was so violent that when I looked down from the narrow and desolate ridge the boundless expanse around and beneath, which suddenly burst upon my sight, overcame me. I felt a mixed sensation of animation and lassitude. Horror and delight such as I scarcely ever before experienced even in the Alps of Switzerland: my spirits almost failed, even curiosity was suspended and I threw myself exhausted upon the ground. These sensations increased during my continuance to the summit. I several times attempted to walk along the ridge but my head became so giddy as I looked down the precipitous sides and particularly towards the great fissure that I could not remain standing.' William Coxe 1799 From 'A historical Tour of Monmouthshire', Volume 1, 1801.

Holy Mountain

Ysgyryd Fawr, Big Skirrid, Holy Mountain are all names given to the lowest of the three great hills that stand sentinel over Abergavenny. It rises 1594 feet (486 metres) above the town, a long ridge whose summit, at its northern extremity, harbours the ruined foundations of a small chapel dedicated to St Michael. The western flank of the ridge is scarred by a large landslide which perhaps occurred soon after the ice age glaciers retreated. This craggy landslide gives the mountain a cloven appearance. The Welsh word 'Ysgyryd', which is not in modern usage, almost certainly means 'split' or 'cloven.'

Ysgyryd Fawr rising above Abergavenny is also known as Holy Mountain

There are many myths and customs surrounding Holy Mountain. One such myth declares that the landslide was caused by the earthquake occurring at the moment of Christ's death on the cross. Another account claims that it happened when Noah's Ark passed over the hill. The red soil of the mountain was said to have been brought here by St Patrick either from Ireland or the Holy Land (there seems to be some doubt but who can be certain after so many years). Farmers collected the red soil from around the mountain on Good Friday and scattered it on their land to ensure a good harvest. The soil was also placed in their coffins prior to burial. The chapel on the hill was in use until at least 1680. For centuries it was a place of pilgrimage. Pope Clement X in 1676 granted plenary indulgence to those visiting the chapel on the Feast of St Michael.

In the vicinity of the chapel, where remains are just visible, there is a monument to an even earlier occupation. It is one of the very many Iron Age hillforts occupying the prominences of the hills in these parts.

Skirrid Mountain, like its westerly neighbour Sugar Loaf, is owned by the National Trust. In recent years the National Trust has acquired more land at both of these sites. On the Skirrid they bought the conifer plantation occupying its south-western lower slope. In time the conifers will be replaced by native broad leafed trees and larch. Meanwhile new tracks have been cut through the plantation. In springtime the flowers, particularly the wood anemones and bluebells, are outstanding.

When you reach the summit with its ruined chapel take time to admire the view. This enjoyment is not always possible. The ridge is very exposed and there are times when progress along it can be arduous against cross winds or head winds. It may not in fact be the windiest spot in Wales but it must be a strong contender.

View towards Sugar Loaf from the summit of Holy Mountain

26

The best way off Skirrid is a little difficult to find. It is by an old track (marked as a footpath on the map) on its eastern side. The track leads off the summit ridge some 220 yards (200 metres) south of the ruined chapel at a point where the surface has been pitted as a result of ancient quarrying.

The track leads down to the mountain fence. Look for a bridle gate and take the footpath across fields heading in a broadly northerly direction. All the footpaths across fields are well marked. Your path takes you down through two fields with a small stream to your left. It then turns sharp left and leads to a stile by an old barn. Cross the stile and then cross another field to the stile leading onto the lane.

When you reach the lane turn right towards Pant-y-tyle and take the first signed footpath on your left. Cross the stile and keeping the hedge to your left walk down through two fields. Go diagonally right in a third field to a stile and enter woodland. Follow the path through the trees, over a bridge and out into the fields again. Continue straight ahead, uphill and bear slightly left to keep a fence line on your right towards Llanfihangel Court.

Llanfihangel Court is a beautifully situated Tudor mansion

When you leave the fields by farm buildings, a left turn takes you onto a rough lane skirting Llanvihangel Court, a fine late 16th century house with a very impressive barn. The drive to the house leads you to the main Hereford-Abergavenny road.

Cross the road and continue up the track then turn right into Llanvihangel Crucorney and should you feel so inclined to the Skirrid Inn.

The Skirrid Inn

There are probably a large number of inns claiming to be the oldest in Wales. But no matter whether the Skirrid Inn can rightly claim this distinction its great antiquity is undisputed. It dates as far back as the 11th century. It was here that the beastly Judge Jeffreys held one of his bloody assizes. The chapel on Skirrid was one of those places where the Catholics held their forbidden rites. One of their number was hanged from a beam above the stairwell of the inn. Time and numerous alterations have changed the exterior and interior of this imposing building but it still has great character and comfort within. At the end of a winter walk when the great hearth is ablaze with a welcome fire, it is as good a place as any to round off the day.

The Skirrid Inn is said to be the oldest pub in Wales

Working on the assumption that you visited the Skirrid Inn, turn left as you come out then left again to take the road signposted to Llanthony. At the bottom of the hill turn right and cross the bridge over the Honddu river. Take the first footpath on your left up to Great Llwygy farm. It is well signed. Take great care crossing the railway line. On reaching the farm turn left and after a short distance, pass through a gateway on the right and take the waymarked path on the right that rises steeply.

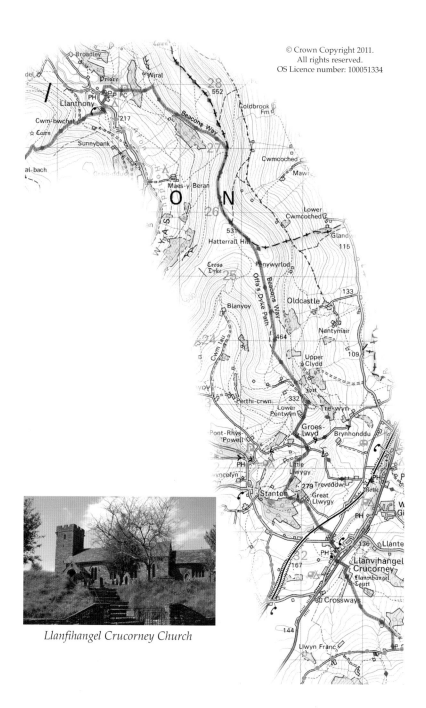

© Crown Copyright 2011.
All rights reserved.
OS Licence number: 100051334

Llanfihangel Crucorney Church

29

On coming out of the wooded area onto open land go diagonally right on the line of a path that drops down to a stile and from that point the route is clear, following a track. It reaches the lane at a gate opposite Trawellwyd. It is on this high section that you get one of the finest views in the National Park. You can see north westwards into the Llanthony Valley and to the southwest you have the view through Cwm Coed y Cerrig towards the mountains above Crickhowell.

On reaching the metalled lane turn left. When you get to the crossroads continue straight ahead and after about 0.5 miles (0.8 km) go through the mountain gate onto Hatterrall Hill to join Offa's Dyke National Trail.

Your route follows the Offa's Dyke path northwards for 2.8 miles (4.5 kms) across the heather moor.

The route follows a section of Offas's Dyke National Trail on Hatterrall Hill

The land you are on is common land which means that there are neighbouring farmers who have rights to graze their livestock here. The track you are on is not only used by walkers but other recreational groups such as pony trekkers,hang-gliders and occasionally the unwelcome, noisy and damaging motor scrambler bikes.

Although the hill is under pressure and in need of repair (for which there is inadequate funding) there is a good chance that you will have it to yourself.

The Offa's Dyke path along the ridge is waymarked by a series Old Red Sandstone milestone-like structures. The stone for these was provided by a small quarry below the Twyn y Gaer hillfort on the ridge west of Hatterrall Hill.

The path from Pentwyn hill fort ascends to a triangulation pillar then drops slightly and rises again to cross the Cwmyoy spur. When it starts to descend, the Llanthony Valley is set out before you with the priory visible in the distance. Proceed along Offa's Dyke Path until just after it starts to rise again. At that point you will see a stone waymarker directing you down to Llanthony to the left and Longtown to the right. Before you make the descent to Llanthony be sure to take the right turn and look down towards Longtown and the panorama before you. To the west is Wales where ridges seem to extend forever. To the east into England is a purely pastoral landscape of farms and green fields ringed in the far distance by the 'blue remembered hills' of Housemann's poem.

It is a gradual and comfortable descent to the priory. Where the route leaves the open hill there is a fingerpost directing you down. You go down a field, through Wiral Wood and emerge from the trees with Llanthony Priory just one field away.

Llanthony Priory in the Vale of Ewyas

"The Vale of Ewyas, more commonly known as the Llanthony Valley, is among the gems in Wales."

A.G. Bradley 1911

Llanthony Priory

Llanthony Priory is a ruin of great beauty in a splendid setting. William de Lacey, a kinsman of a local Norman baron, came across the site about 1103 when out hunting in the area. There was then, near the present priory, a ruined hermit's cell perhaps dating from 500 AD said to be founded by St David himself. (Llanthony gets its name from a contraction of the Welsh Llan Ddewi Nant Honddu – Church of David on the river Honddu) The ruined chapel inspired William de Lacey to embark on a project which resulted in the foundation of an Augustinian Priory on this site.

The priory was built in stages. In 1103 Ernisius, Chaplain to Queen Matilda, joined William de Lacey and they gathered around them a community of men who had chosen the monastic life. In 1108 a church dedicated to St John the Baptist was consecrated. By 1118 the community had become an Augustinian house funded by both Queen Matilda and King Henry I. Such is a brief account of how it all started.

The order suffered many vicissitudes. In 1135 a serious Welsh uprising began. The canons fled from Llanthony. First they went to Hereford and then moved on to Gloucester where they established another priory which they named Llanthony Secunda. They did not return to Llanthony until about 1175 when, with generous endowments from Irish estates, they began work erecting a church to replace the 1108 building. It was from 1175 to 1190 that work began on the buildings whose ruins we see today. The building work was completed between 1200 and 1230.

Six hundred years later in 1807 the priory came into the news when Walter Savage Landor bought the Llanthony Estate that had come into existence at the time of the Reformation. Walter Savage Landor was a writer much respected by other writers in his day. He was a friend of Dickens and the Brownings. He lived from 1775 to 1864 but his time as master of Llanthony extended only from 1807 to 1813.

His time there was short but action packed. His efforts to set up a school at Llanthony were thwarted by the Church. The building of a fine house was made near impossible by jerry-builders and the theft of materials. He employed lawyers who took fees and did little work. He was robbed by agents of the Prince of Wales of a fine flock of Merino sheep intended for Llanthony and could obtain no redress. He railed against local corruption without effect. Being unable to interest the proper authorities in the corrupt practices he named a name. He wrote and distributed a handbill through towns in the locality. The named man sued for libel and won the case and Landor had £800 damages to pay. His family took over the management of the estate and he fled to Italy to avoid paying the exorbitant damages.

The estate remained in the Landor family until the second half of the 20th century. The last agent for the estate bought the priory and the Abbey Hotel when it finally went up for sale. The ruin and the hotel remain in private ownership but CADW is responsible for the maintenance of the Priory.

The 'Abbey Hotel', Llanthony

DAY TWO
Llanthony to Crickhowell

Distance: 12 miles / 19.5 km
Ascent: 3,063 feet / 934 metres   Map: Explorer OL13

THIS part of the trail crosses three of the Black Mountains four main ridges and provides (if you are blessed by good weather) spectacular views of the Honddu, Grwyne Fawr, Grwyne Fechan and the Usk valleys. Additionally, you will have the chance to see most of the highest points in the Black Mountains. This walk is a great favourite of those who know the Black Mountains well.

The route starts at the hamlet of Llanthony at the junction of the approach road to the priory and the road from Llanvihangel Crucorney to Capel-y-ffin. There is a metal finger post directing you to 'Bal-Bach 2km' pointing you in the direction of a group of houses and outbuildings.

Llanthony Priory from Cwm Bwchel

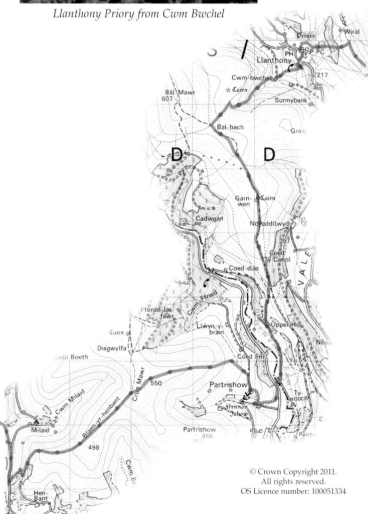

© Crown Copyright 2011.
All rights reserved.
OS Licence number: 100051334

The path you require goes in front of this house and leads to a metal bridge over the Honddu River. Cross the bridge and then take the first stile on your right and take the fenced off path up to the next stile. Cross the stile and then the little stream and follow the waymarked route up through the field. At the top of the field a stile leads into a wet area of rough woodland. You will come to a wooden signpost at which you take the path to Cwm Bwchel. After crossing a wooden bridge you leave the rough woodland behind you and enter a field with a way marked footpath leading you up to the farmhouse named Cwm-bwchel.

To the right of the farmhouse the path rises steeply to the top of the field where a stile leads into a conifer plantation. Continue straight ahead. Another stile leads onto the hill just beyond which there is a fingerpost. You take the steeply climbing path up to Bal-Bach. The stream is in a deepening valley to your left. Continue upwards for about 0.6 miles (1km) pausing often to look back over the valley you have left. Eventually the path meets another track. Turn left and continue up to the ridge.

Once you reach the ridge there is a panoramic view of the Black Mountains. The Skirrid, to the south-east, looks particularly good as does its near neighbour Sugar Loaf. You are also standing on very fine heather moorland which is being very well managed and cared for by its owner.

On reaching the ridge you turn left and take the well-used track that goes in a south-easterly direction. From hereon it is downhill for the next 2.5 miles (4 km), making the steep climb you have just made all the more worthwhile.

The main path leads to Garn-Wen which is a small tower like dry stone structure of relatively modern date built from the stones of the large Early Bronze Age cairn on which it rests.

From this cairn the route proceeds downhill and reaches a point just south of an area marked as Coed Mawr on the map just after the forest plantation on your left. There is a small rough pile of stones in the centre of the main track supporting a stump of carved stone.

The Stone of Vengeance
This fragment of carved stone may be the remnant of a medieval pilgrims' cross. Alternatively it may be, as is popularly believed, a monument commemorating the assassination of Richard de Clare in 1135. It is known locally as the Stone of Vengeance – Dial Cerrig. The story is that Richard de Clare was making his way from Abergavenny Castle to his property in

Talgarth when he and his party was attacked and slain by Morgan-ap-Owen (the Welsh Lord of Caerleon) and his followers. It was an act of revenge for which the Welsh had very good cause.

Garn Wen

The Stone of Vengeance

Proceed from the Vengeance Stone by leaving the broad track that you have been using. Turn sharp right and follow the line of the wall keeping the wall on your left and you will reach a gate that leads onto a track between two walls. Go through the gate and follow the track down to Upper House farm and then the metalled road down to Ty- mawr farm.

Ty- mawr

Ty-mawr is one of many very old houses that are to be found in the Black Mountains. The house we see today together with its three storey barn, built into the steep bank, dates from the early 17th century. Prior to that period an older house existed that was set at right angles to the northern end of the present building. It was built circa 1500 and the present building was put there as an extension to the original. Circa 1600 there would have been a T-shaped building on this site. All that remains of the early building is its substantial porch. This is incorporated into the newer building and now serves as a large walk-in pantry with some of its original features as a porch intact.

The older building became known when the present owner uncovered the foundations whilst carrying out essential drainage work. It was only then that the full extent of the original building emerged.

Two substantial 13 feet (4 m) high retaining dry stone walls have been rebuilt. The one at the back of the house was covered by earth and was revealed during the excavations. It dates from 1500 and has been restored to its original style.

Continue down the lane beyond Ty-mawr and pass the Tabernacle Chapel then cross the bridge over the Grwyne Fawr river. The lane rises steeply from the river to the main Grwyne Fawr road. (Local people pronounce this word as 'griney' as in tiny and fower as in power).

For some 20 years at the beginning of the 20th century a light- gauge railway made its way from Llanvihangel Crucorney up to the reservoir workings at the top of the valley. A temporary village was built there to house the workers and their families.

The reservoir inevitably flooded farmland. The extensive forestry plantations within the valley destroyed many other farms. Farming in this valley had long been in decline. The forester who oversaw the planting of trees here had farmed in the valley. It is to his credit that he took care to plant the trees around the farmhouses in such a way that their ruins would remain a fitting testament to the generations who had lived and laboured here. Forty seven ruined farms have been discovered and researched and their known histories pieced together. The work will in time be published and give us some idea of what went on in this now depopulated area.

Opposite the point where the chapel lane meets the road you will see the stile which you must cross. Follow the waymarked path that takes you up across the fields to another historic house. As you approach the house head for the gate just to the left of it. The route takes you in front of the house.

Tyn-y-Llwyn Farmhouse

Tyn-y-Llwyn

Whereas Ty-mawr has only recently been discovered Tyn-y-Llwyn has the distinction of being named in Gothic script on the Ordnance Survey map. According to Richard Haslam, in the Powys volume of Buildings of Wales (Penguin 1979), it dates from the 15th and 16th century and was converted into its present cross shape in 1649. The house remained in the same family for four hundred years until its recent sale. The house possesses many unaltered interior features. To the walker approaching it from the fields below it is the splendid yew topiary which first strikes the eye. Next it is the recently restored stone tiled roofs. Having taken in the fine house itself the enormous flagstones, that form the terrace, make you wonder what giants of men once worked here.

Having passed the house turn sharp right and walk up by the garden wall through a gate that leads into a field. The well-defined field track rises up the field before dividing. Turn left and head up to the church.

Partrishow Church

Partrishow Church

A Latin inscription around the rim of this church's simple stone font reads.
'MENHIR ME FECIT I TEPORE GENILLIN'
Making allowances for the bad spelling of the 11th century stonemason it may be translated as:
MENHIR (the name of the mason) MADE ME
AT THE TIME OF GENILLIN

38

Genillin was a Welsh prince who died circa 1065. This indicates that there was a church here around that date. All that remains of the original building would appear to be the north and south walls of the present nave.

According to tradition this church commemorates a Celtic saint whose name might have been Ishow or Issue and whose history is unknown. It is believed that a shrine existed here prior to the building of the church. This would have been a site of pilgrimage and the nearby Holy Well would have made the location doubly important. The western end of the church is walled off from the nave and the chancel and is described as an Eglwys y bedd; literally 'church of the grave'. It is possible that the remains of the saint lie beneath the altar in this separate chapel that may have originally held the saint's shrine.

On entering the church through the 14th century porch one is at first struck by its freshness and its light. Then one by one the special features emerge. First there is the simple but imposing font and behind it on the west wall the ochre painting of a Doom figure. The north wall carries a royal coat of arms and, together with the south wall, some beautifully executed texts from the Bible, the latter with corrections inserted.

The magnificent rood screen (circa 1500) is justly celebrated as are the Brute memorials that decorate the walls of the much restored Elizabethan chancel.

The 16th century rood screen in Partrishow Church is quite remarkable

The Brutes were a family of farmers and monumental masons who, over several generations, lived and worked in the village of Llanbedr some 3 miles (5 km) southwest of the church. Their monuments are characterised by the use of brilliantly coloured dyes. The decorative motifs are flamboyant and baroque. The lettering is particularly elegant. Tulips are amongst the preferred floral decorations and cherubs abound. On the north wall of the chancel the blue robed angels are blowing golden trumpets with eyes bulging because of the effort. In other churches the Victorian vicars found such monuments as these too cheerfully vulgar and had them removed from the walls. Here at Partrishow they have kept everything.

When you leave the church going up the steps by the west wall note the stone tiled building with the mounting steps. Within that building there was a small fireplace so that the parson could dry his wet clothes during the service.

Although the church is remote it is still in regular use as the fresh floral decorations invariably attest. It is much visited by walkers who time their arrival for the middle of the day and sit on the stone south-facing bench (circa 1300) to enjoy their lunch.

On leaving the church turn right and right again to go up the stone steps between the west wall of the church and the stone outbuilding to the stile at the top of the bank. Cross the stile and turn right, then continue along the lane until you see a waymarked bridleway branching left off the road. Take the bridleway on the left and continue upwards. When you have passed through the gate onto the open hill you will see in front of you a small enclosed area used as a sheep-fold. Continue ahead through the enclosed area and leave it by the gate against the dry stone wall. When you leave the enclosure turn left and follow the fence line up. A wall replaces the fence line and shortly after this the track divides. Take the right fork, and at the next junction continue ahead following a waymark post. After 0.75 miles (1.2km) along a well defined path you will reach a triangulation pillar.

Continue ahead and descend to a bridleway. Turn left and follow the track as it contours around Blaen-yr-henbant then descend to follow a field boundary on your left to a metal gate. Take the smaller wooden gate on the right and descend at first straight on then bearing right to a field boundary. Keep the field boundary on your right and continue down to the road.

When you reach the road turn right and continue on the lane, until on your left you will see a stile. Cross the stile into the field and take the waymarked route down passing to the left of Llwynon. As the path descends you will see to your left the wooden bridge over the Grwyne Fechan.

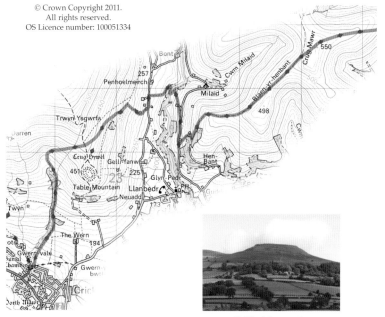

© Crown Copyright 2011.
All rights reserved.
OS Licence number: 100051334

Table Mountain

Cross the bridge and the way up is well waymarked. After a steep ascent in a more or less northerly direction the path hairpins round and proceeds in a southerly direction before veering west over a stile then diagonally upwards to the top left hand corner of the field onto the road.

On reaching the road turn left. After about 220 yards (200 metres) turn right at the house shown as Green Cottage on the map. The path goes up until, after a ruined barn and by a small conifer plantation, a gate leads onto the open hill. Go through the gate and turn right and walk a short way until you see a well trodden track leading upwards to your left. This path will take you towards Table Mountain (Crug Hwyel). When the bracken is up it is not so easy to take a direct route to Table Mountain but you will easily find your way there. On reaching Table Mountain climb the crag onto its summit.

There is an Iron Age hillfort on the summit of Crug Hwyel. You will have crossed the substantial ditch dug as part of its defences. Crug Hwyel commands extensive views over the Usk Valley but having no supply of water it could not survive a siege. However, within the fort there would have been a number of dwellings and perhaps buildings serving other purposes. Such hillforts abound in the National Park. To either side of the Usk Valley they are particularly in evidence together with other less grand enclosures which may be of this date.

The route to Crickhowell is downhill all the way. Leave Table Mountain in a northerly direction and follow the mountain wall that curves round to the west. The route follows a well used track that stays fairly close to the wall until, at the bottom of the cwm / valley, you will find a bridleway, to your left coming onto the hill through sheepfolds. Go through the sheepfolds and take the track between very substantial stone walls. For a short length the route is on the same line as the stream. When it has been wet this can present a small problem. It is usually possible to keep your feet dry by moving to raised stones by the wall on your right before crossing the stream to a low bank on the left hand side. The path leads to an attractive upland pasture. Continue down this pasture to enter the woodland of Cwm Cumbeth. Walk downwards keeping the stream to your right until you eventually arrive at some stables and a modern barn. Just to the left of the stables you will see a gate and a stile. Cross the stile and go right and walk to Gwernvale Lane. At the junction you can turn left for the A40 and Crickhowell to end this section of the walk or right to continue with the Beacons Way.

Crickhowell's 13-arched bridge and Table Mountain in the background

Crickhowell

The official guide to the Brecon Beacons National Park published in 1967 by Her Majesty's Stationery Office begins thus:

CRICKHOWELL. *A small, sheltered, market town set between the lower slopes of Crucywel (Table Mountain) and the Usk. The first local fortress was the Iron Age camp on Crucywel and the first Norman castle may have been on the roadside mound a mile north-west of the town. The main medieval castle in Crickhowell controlled a large area but now only its motte and bailey, parts of the curtain wall and a small round tower survive. Porth Mawr, on the west side of the town, is the great gate of a Tudor house of the Herbert family. The parish church of St Edmund, founded in the fourteenth century, contains much nineteenth century work. The pleasing thirteen arched and strongly buttressed bridge over the Usk was rebuilt in 1810. Gwernvale just north-west of Crickhowell, was the home of Sir George Everest.'*

In 1804 Richard Fenton called Crickhowell ' the most cheerful looking town I ever saw'. In a way that says it all and 200 years later it is still true. The town looks very good indeed. There is a delightful jumble of buildings, prettily painted, many of which were built in the late eighteenth and early nineteenth century. Others, although possessing pleasing more modern exteriors, have interiors of greater antiquity. It also has shops still owned by local families and the familiar fascades of the average High Street are nowhere to be seen. You can eat and drink well here.

The Bear Hotel in Crickhowell is an old coaching inn

DAY THREE
Crickhowell to Llangynidr
Distance to Llangynidr : 12.2 miles / 19.5 km
Ascent: 2,230 feet / 680 metres   Map: OS Explorer OL 13

THIS route explores the western flank of Pen Cerrig-calch and Pen Gloch-y-pibwr before crossing the Rhiangol valley at Cwmdu and making the climb onto Mynydd Llangorse. It is a less arduous day than the two preceding sections of the trail. The route to Cwmdu has been chosen because it is so beautiful and presents an ever changing landscape which has the capacity to surprise. There is a tendency amongst hill walkers to stick to the ridges. High level routes are very exciting whereas the views offered from mountain wall levels often have exceptional qualities denied to those who prefer to keep their heads in or nearer to the clouds.

The walk commences from just before the White Hart public house on the A40 at the junction of Gwernvale and Pregge Lane (SO 216192).

The metalled lane continues beyond Gwernvale Farm until, at a gate it suddenly changes its character and is replaced by a track, ingeniously made of concrete sleepers, leading to Twyn. Just before you get to Twyn cross the stile on your right into the field and head up to a ruined barn. Go through a broken wall keeping the barn on your left and continue straight ahead. At a track junction, head for a metal gate (in a stone wall) which you will see to your left. Then continue straught ahead, keeping the stone wall on your right. Walk on between two stone walls and cross a stile into an open green area. Bear right again and continue upwards between stone walls to reach a metal gate which leads you onto the open hill.

Follow the path to the left which shortly leads uphill to reach the corner of a conifer plantation above Foxhall. There are excellent views across the Usk Valley from here.

Continue walking just above the hill fence which contours around the hill for about 900 yards (1000 metres). At this point the fence line changes direction and drops almost directly downhill. Instead of following the fence take a waymarked track to your right that will drop quite sharply to rejoin the hill wall about 200 yards north of Cwm Mawr Cottage. This wall eventually turns sharp left. At that point go straight ahead on the obvious track that crosses a stream, turns left and rises for a while. The path very soon connects with the mountain wall again.

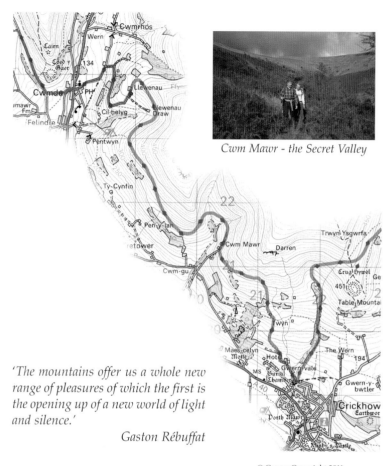

Cwm Mawr - the Secret Valley

'The mountains offer us a whole new range of pleasures of which the first is the opening up of a new world of light and silence.'

Gaston Rébuffat

© Crown Copyright 2011.
All rights reserved.
OS Licence number: 100051334

A Secret Valley?

It is surprising how little known this cwm is. It is not particularly remote but the direct routes to it, involve risking life and limb on the A40 which has neither path nor verge alongside it. This steep sided south facing valley is surely a very special place and like many other places in the Black Mountain, it is inaccessible. Perhaps we should rejoice that such places exist and are only known to a few locals and the energetic explorers of the hills. This inaccessibility has resulted in the hawthorn bushes bearing an abundance of mistletoe which has not found its way to market.

In winter and spring sunshine, when the hawthorn is still bare of leaves, the bushes appear to be crowned with a golden halo of yellow mistletoe leaves.

Follow the wall to the next stream. Cross the stream and turn left to take the track that leaves the boundary line of the wall to climb in a just west of south direction before meeting up with the wall again. The track then contours the hill following the boundary wall. At a point where a small stream crosses the path the boundary wall turns a corner and goes downhill.

Until recently the walker had to lose height here and follow the hill boundary line. In recent years the graziers have cut a broad swathe through the bracken and in so doing have provided an ideal route for walkers. So you simply carry on straight ahead through the line of the cut bracken, until in due course, the boundary wall/fence line track is re-encountered. The contouring continues for about a mile in a north westerly direction. Then, it descends into a cwm, at the bottom of which is a farmhouse called Llewenau Draw and the direction changes to northeast. Do not take the path off the hill at this point, but continue to follow the mountain wall up the other side of the cwm until you arrive at a stile (SO 191238) which leads across a field to another stiile. Continue down across rough ground to reach the driveway to Llewenau and then turn left to a metalled road that leads to the village of Cwmdu where there is a pub, church and cafe.

Cwmdu in the Rhiangoll Valley

Cwmdu Church

St. Michael's church, like Partrishow, dates back to the 11th century. However, when in 1831 the church was rebuilt much of the older fabric dating from around 1430, was lost. In 1907 further rebuilding took place. Despite all this reconstruction some interesting features survive. Incorporated into the south buttress is a stone of great antiquity. It dates from the late 6th or early 7th century and is inscribed with the words CATACUS HIS JACIT/FILIUS TEGERNACUS (*Here lies Catacus, son of Terganacus*) as well as Ogham inscriptions.

© Crown Copyright 2011.
All rights reserved.
OS Licence number: 100051334

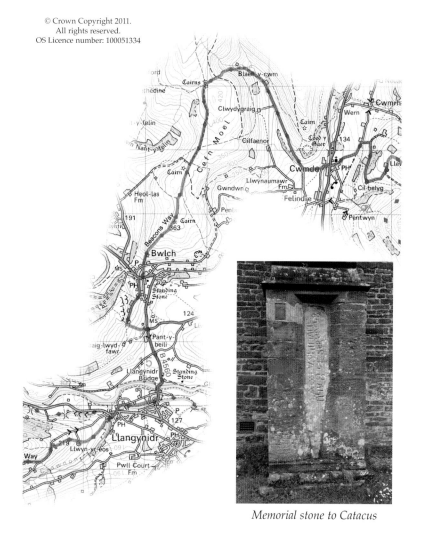

Memorial stone to Catacus

This church is especially remembered because in the 19th century the vicar in charge was Thomas Price, a bard, antiquary and scholar of the Welsh language and history. He pioneered the teaching of the Welsh language at a time when its study was forbidden in schools.

Directly opposite the pub, on the other side of the main road, there is a lane. Walk down this lane and immediately after crossing the bridge you will see on your right, a stile into a field. Two paths set off from this stile. Take the one that heads for the top left-hand corner of the field. Cross that stile, turn right and continue along the hedge line until a gate leads onto a lane.

On reaching the lane turn right and continue along it for about 1.25 miles (2km) up to Blaen-y-cwm-uchaf farm at the head of the valley. At that point a bridlegate to your left leads onto the open hill. Go through the gate, turn right and take the track which climbs steeply upwards and connects with a north south bridleway across the hill. Turn left. (It is worth remarking that there are more tracks on the hill than are shown on the map).

Bwlch, your next destination, lies at the southern end of this bridleway, and as you proceed along it Llangorse Lake will come into view.

Llangorse is the largest natural lake in South Wales

Llangorse Lake

Llangorse Lake was formed in the Ice Age by a giant glacial scoop. It is entirely natural and was, even in historic times, somewhat larger than it is now. The Official Guide to The National Park published in 1967 states

48

This beautifully set lake is best seen from the surrounding hills', which is as true today as it was then. William Condrey, the naturalist writing in 1981, was very gloomy indeed about this lake. He was of the view then that it should be a National Nature Reserve to better protect its flora and fauna which was then being ravaged by all manner of polluting agents, as well as the water sports, including speed boats, which were likely to be damaging the habitats.

It is one thing to say that speed boats and noisy youths and kids enjoying themselves have a damaging affect on the wildlife and plants but it is quite another thing to prove it. In fairness the owner of the lake has done much to reduce the impact of 'unsustainable activities'. Furthermore, the National Park Authority has managed to acquire a large section of the southern shore of the lake so things are moving in the right direction.

The route you take hugs the fence and wall line until it drops down into a sort of funnel just above Bwlch. You come off the hill by a long white house set at a right angle to the track. Go down the rough metalled road beside the house. When you reach the T junction turn right and go a few paces then turn left onto a footpath going down between two stone walls. It leads to a chapel and its graveyard. Go through the graveyard and just below you is the A40.

Your intended destination is Llangynidr so cross the A 40 (with great care) turn right and just after the New Inn public house you will see on your left Darren Road. Go along Darren Road until you see a waymarked path on your left. Follow the path, cross two stiles and turn sharp right to walk along the edge of the field and pass through a gateway. Then turn left going downhill through a quaint iron gate and over a stile beside farm buildings to the road. Follow the road downhill with great care into Llangynidr.

You enter Llangynidr by crossing a superb ancient narrow stone bridge. Continue a little way up the hill and join the canal and head west as far as lock 65.

Llangynidr

Llangynidr is a mixture of the old and the new. But it is a village intensely aware of its past. In the year 2000 the Llangynidr Local History Society published 'Shadows in a Landscape. Llangynidr. The Evolution of a Community.' This is a 300 page, lavishly illustrated, account of the history of the village and the surrounding area. It is a model local history text.

In the summer of 2002 an excavation organised and financed by the villagers themselves uncovered the remains of a small Norman castle. Another village project arising out of the Millennium was the restoration of an impressive length of dry stone Walling that separated the common land from the farmed land on the mountainous terrain to the south of the village. That work is still in progress.

Llangynidr Bridge spanning the river Usk

What the casual visitor is most aware of in the village is the river Usk with its splendid, but very narrow bridge, built between 1587 and 1630 and the canal. The Brecon and Abergavenny Canal came to the village in the late 1790s. At that time, as 'Shadows in a Landscape' records, the village had a population of 200 but as many as 600 workers were employed building the canal. We can only imagine what impact that must have had on the community. The purpose of the canal, which extended eventually from Pontypool to Brecon, was to bring coal and agricultural lime into the heart of rural Breconshire.

The hills to the south of Llangynidr are capped by carboniferous limestone which further south again is capped by millstone grit. This limestone was extensively quarried along the southern rim of what is now the National Park. Sometimes limekilns were built on the quarry site and the lime produced would have been shifted down by mule cart. With the coming of the canal, tram roads (horse drawn) were constructed to take limestone down to the canalside limekilns as well as take the stone to the valleys ironworks where it was used as a flux. These same tram roads were used to transport coal down to the canal and in some cases iron products were brought to the canal for shipment to South Wales.

DAY FOUR
Llangynidr to Storey Arms

    Distance: 14.2 miles / 22.7 km
    Ascent: 3,345 feet / 1020 m   Maps: OS Explorer OL13 & 12

THIS is perhaps the most demanding day of the whole route. A prompt start is advised. This section of the trail takes you through the Eastern Beacons and into the Central Beacons. Rather inconveniently it starts on Brecon Beacons Eastern Area map and moves onto the Central and Western Area map. The landscape becomes exposed and in bad weather can be very wild and inhospitable. There are three significant climbs. The first from Llangynidr to Bwlch-y-waun, just south of Tor y Foel, is relatively gradual. The second from Torpantau is very much steeper and demanding. The third up to the summit of Pen y Fan is steep and coming at the end of the day is the most severe.

© Crown Copyright 2011.
All rights reserved.
OS Licence number: 100051334

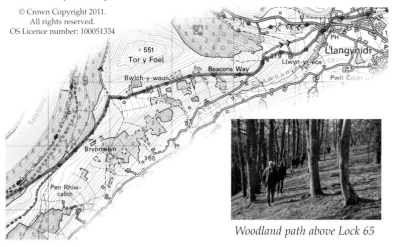

Woodland path above Lock 65

    The start of the route begins at the canal at Lock 65 (east of the road bridge over the canal) at the western end of the village. Cross the canal by the wooden bridge at the lower lock gate and take the track immediately ahead that rises through woodland. A stile leads into a field and the waymarked path is straight ahead. To aim directly for the stile on the opposite side of the field head for the power line post in the centre of the field and the position of the stile in the hedgerow will be clearly visible. Turn right in the next field and follow the waymarked route uphill across fields by Llwyn-yr-êos farm to Pen-y-beili farm.

Turn left on reaching the lane at Pen-y-bailey and walk about 300 yards (300 m) along the lane. Then turn right onto the signposted bridleway that rises steadily up to Bwlch-y-waun farm and continues beyond the farm as a metalled road. This road meets up with the lane from Talybont at a gate in a beautifully restored dry stone wall. Go through the gate and pause to reflect on what lies before you.

Reservoirs and Forests

Talybont Reservoir lies below. It is one of sixteen reservoirs in the Brecon Beacons National Park. Most were built in the late 19th and early 20th centuries to support the increasing population and industrialisation of South Wales. This reservoir dates from 1927 and it supplies water to Newport and towns and villages along its route. The reservoir has become, along with Llangorse Lake, an important habitat for wintering water birds. Amongst these are goosander, widgeon, tufted duck, pochard, golden eye and mute swan. Bewick's and whooper swans are known winter visitors.

As you can see a large area of forestry surrounds the lake. The combination of forests and reservoirs transformed the landscape of the Brecon Beacons National Park during the 20th century. The planting of these coniferous forests has been controversial. Recent years have seen changes in the Forestry Commission's policies. Open access is very much the order of the day and a large number of forest trails have been created. Throughout the National Park walkers and less energetic visitors have benefited from the car parks, picnic sites and other facilities that the forest authorities have provided.

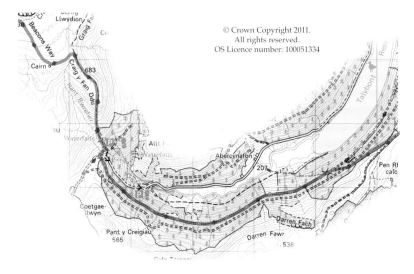

© Crown Copyright 2011.
All rights reserved.
OS Licence number: 100051334

Talybont Reservoir from Bwlch-y-waun

Having gone through the gate to Bwlch-y-waun farm you turn left and walk along the road for about 1 mile (1.6km) until you reach the point shown on the map as Pen Rhiw-calch. Here you will find a memorial bench (on which to rest and enjoy the view) and a fingerpost pointing down through the forest to Abercynafon.

The Bryn Oer (or Ore) Tramroad
Benjamin Hall (of Big Ben fame) built, in 1815, a tramroad eight miles long to connect the canal at Talybont with the Rhymney Ironworks at Trefil. The lane on which you have been walking goes over the line of this old tramroad. If you look before going down to Abercynafon you can see where the track went under the road.

The fingerpost to Abercynafon points your way down through the forest. About halfway down the path crosses the eastern route of the Taff Trail which, for the benefit of cyclists and walkers, links Cardiff to Brecon.

Turn left along the Taff Trail and take this gradually ascending route through the forest. After 2.5 miles (4km) it emerges from the forest and connects with the narrow mountain road that links Talybont-on-Usk with Merthyr Tydfil.

On reaching the road turn right and after a short while you will see a track on your left leading to a car park. Head for the car park and immediately you have crossed a culverted stream with an attractive waterfall you will see on your left, just before the entrance to the car park, the route up.

The path starts by following the forest fence to the right and a series of waterfalls on the left. The route up needs no description or guide. The constructed pitched stone path leaves no doubt of the way to go.

When you reach the top of the steep ascent of Craig y Fan Ddu take the track that follows the eastern edge of the summit spur. After about half a mile (800 m) you will reach the point where the Blaen Caerfanell stream plunges over the cliff face. Do not cross the stream but turn left and follow the track that takes a compass bearing of 190 degrees. After about 100 yards (90 m) the track forks. Take the right hand higher track that continues on a general 220 degrees bearing. The track begins to bear right. After another 100 yards (100m) it is on a 250 degrees bearing. About 330 yards (300 m) from the fork in the track it crosses a small stream and (on a bearing that has veered to 290 degrees) after about 110 yards (100m) arrives at a small cairn.

© Crown Copyright 2011.
All rights reserved.
OS Licence number: 100051334

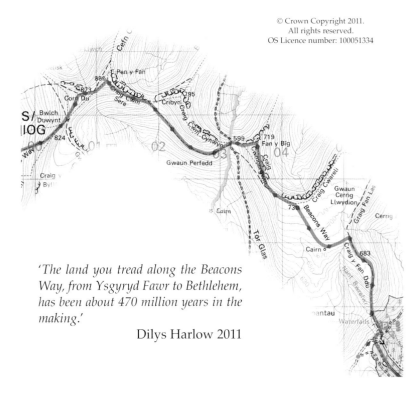

'The land you tread along the Beacons Way, from Ysgyryd Fawr to Bethlehem, has been about 470 million years in the making.'

Dilys Harlow 2011

From this cairn the track takes a general compass bearing of 320 degrees across Gwaun Cerrig Llwydion avoiding all the peaty and boggy ground to the right. Regular users have marked the route with small cairns along the first length of the route to Craig Cwmoergwm escarpment. Just before reaching the escarpment the track veers left to run parallel to it. At this point leave the track and stride out the 22 yards (20m) to the escarpment path. Having reached the escarpment the route is well defined.

The summits from left to right are: Corn Du, Pen y Fan and Cribyn

Your route to Pen y Fan is in a north-westerly direction along the cliff tops above Cwm Oergwm around to Fan y Big to see the view from the protruding rock at its summit known as the 'Diving Board'. From the summit of Fan y Big drop down to the pass that is known as the 'Gap Road'.

In this part of the Central Beacons the National Park Authority has carried out extensive work on the paths to repair the scars that the thousands of stamping feet have inflicted on the hills. The main technique used is stone pitching which involves driving stones into the hill to produce an effect similar to cobbling. Ideally the stone should be local to blend in with the terrain. If it has to be imported it should be stone of the same type and appearance as the local stone wherever possible. More often than not the stone has to be flown in by helicopter.

The National Trust owns the high land to the west of Fan y Big as far as the Merthyr to Brecon road. Over the years it has had a rolling programme of erosion repair work. This is carried out by well supervised and trained volunteers who are based in the hostel style accommodation at Blaenglyn, the headquarters of the National Trust in this part of Wales. If you feel like a working holiday get in touch with the National Trust at Blaenglyn. (Telephone 01874 622264)

The Diving Board on Fan y Big

Miss out Cribyn by taking the well used track around its base. Since to climb it would result in too late a finish to your day. The climb to the summit of Pen y Fan is a strenuous affair.

Pen y Fan is ascended via Craig Cwm Sere

Pen y Fan

Pen y Fan is the highest point in South Wales and South Britain. Due to its height and its proximity to a main road it is almost certainly the most climbed peak in South Wales. Furthermore, the walk up from Pont ar Daf on the A470 is relatively gradual and people of a wide range of ability and experience are able to get to the summit. But here, as elsewhere, when the weather turns nasty it can be very challenging. In high winds the summit can be very difficult to approach.

Fifty years ago the way to the summit was not nearly so well defined. The summit was covered with grass and the now crumbling eastern approach to Pen y Fan was hardly eroded at all. It should also be mentioned that public transport access to the Beacons was much better than today. It was then possible to catch a train in Cardiff or Newport and travel to the railway station at Torpantau, four miles south of Pen y Fan. It was possible to walk to the Beacons summits and then descend to Pont ar Daf for a nourishing meal at the café at Storey Arms. From there it was by bus back to Merthyr and down the valleys to Cardiff or Newport. Both the train and the café have gone!

Along the route of the Beacons Way you will have passed very many cairns dating from the Early Bronze Age. About four thousand years ago the climate of Britain was much warmer than today and many of the upland ridges would have been under cultivation or would have provided good grazing or hunting. The peaks of these hills and mountains were often chosen as burial sites for what might have been the more important members of the peoples who resided here.

Pen y Fan, Corn Du and Fan y Big each had a cairn on their summit. Most of the prominent Bronze Age cairns were pillaged by treasure hunters many years ago. To add insult to injury that on Pen y Fan had a triangulation pillar erected on top of it. Visitor pressure upon the cairn was seriously damaging what remained of it so an excavation took place in 1991 to establish its structure and obtain dating material.

View from summit of Pen y Fan towards Cribyn

© Crown Copyright 2011.
All rights reserved.
OS Licence number: 100051334

After the summit of Pen y Fan the remaining Beacons summit, Corn Du, is but a gentle stroll across from the high point of the Beacons Way.

From the summit of the Beacons there are three ways down to the main road. After a good day out in the hills you will have earned yourself the privilege of taking the shortest route down. From Corn Du summit use the track that leads southwards off its crag to Bwlch Duwynt. From there take the main track ('the motor way') down to the Pont ar Daf car park.

Footbridge spanning the Taf Fawr at Pont ar Daf

On reaching the car park (with toilets and burger van) turn right and after leaving the car park walk northwards along the road to a large white building still called Storey Arms. You will be sorry to learn that it is not a pub but now an Outdoor Education Centre. The old pub of that name was further south on the A470.

If you require accommodation at this location then Llwyn y Celyn Youth Hostel may be reached by following a broad track (a section of the Taff Trail) leading down into Glyn Tarell. A waymarked permitted footpath leads via a footbridge to the hostel.

Note: There is a regular bus service between Merthyr and Brecon that can be boarded at Storey Arms. There is also a more restricted service on Sundays.

DAY FIVE

Fforest Fawr:
Storey Arms to Craig-y-nos Country Park

    Distance: 14.75 miles / 23.7 Km
    Ascent: 1,820 feet / 555 metres   Map: OS Explorer 12

Pen y Fan (and its associated peaks) is certainly the busiest and most often visited upland area in the National Park. By contrast, those hills to the west of the Brecon-Merthyr road, although equally accessible, receive little attention from visitors. This area is frequented by walkers anxious to get away from it all who prefer to have a mountain to themselves rather than share it with all and sundry. You are likely to spend the whole day out and see very few people indeed.

Be warned! Although a large part of the route is on well-defined tracks there are some sections where this is not the case. The ability to read a map and use a compass is essential.

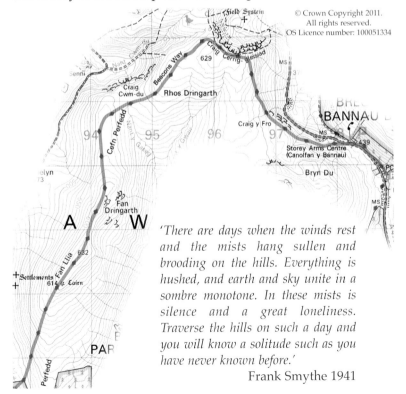

© Crown Copyright 2011.
All rights reserved.
OS Licence number: 100051334

'There are days when the winds rest and the mists hang sullen and brooding on the hills. Everything is hushed, and earth and sky unite in a sombre monotone. In these mists is silence and a great loneliness. Traverse the hills on such a day and you will know a solitude such as you have never known before.'

Frank Smythe 1941

Leave the Storey Arms car park (opposite the Education Centre) by the gate. Bear diagonally right 280 degrees ascending to a well defined path that contours Craig y Fro.

Looking back towards Storey Arms and the summit of Corn Du

Proceed for approximately 1 hour, crossing several streams and taking time to enjoy wonderful views north towards Brecon until you see a fence with a ruined wall behind it. Bear left and ascend keeping the fence on your right. You will then descend to a metal gate with a stile on either side. Turn left and follow the fence line to the right and until you see a good track moving away from the fence line and gently rising on your left. The track is on a general bearing of 230 degrees. Follow this track and where it peters out (across wetter ground) try to keep to this bearing.

This bearing leads to Cefn Perfedd. You will, depending on the wetness of the land, need to pick your way through or round the streams that flow into the Nant y Gaseg. When you reach the shoulder of Cefn Perfedd you will see a faint track leading due south towards Fan Dringarth. This track becomes clearer as you proceed southwards and upwards. The summit of Fan Llia is almost 2 miles (3.2km) away but the gradual ascent with fine views all round makes this one of the most relaxing climbs you could wish for.

When you eventually reach the summit (there is a rough cairn marking it) you will see the track you must take leading down in a southwesterly direction. Unfortunately this track does not take you all the way down. You will need to find your own route skirting the heads of the streams that flow off the hill until you are nearing the fence line.

At the bottom of the hill cross a stile, turn right and proceed to a bridge, car park and picnic site.

Cross the bridge and climb up the steep car park access road to join the Heol Senni (Senni Road) to Ystradfellte road at the top. Turn right and take the next turning on your left which is signed Sarn Helen.

"This is a grim inhospitable land, uninhabited and awesome, yet with its own strange perverse beauty."
Tudor Edwards 1950

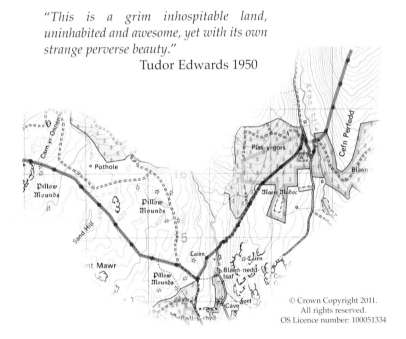

© Crown Copyright 2011.
All rights reserved.
OS Licence number: 100051334

Sarn Helen
This Roman road or causeway (sarn) is reputed to have been named after the 4th century Princess Elen of Segontium, wife of the Emperor Maximus. However, it was constructed much earlier to link a Roman fort in the Usk Valley (Y Gaer near Brecon), built around AD 80, with a fort at Neath (Nidvm), 30 miles to the south-west.

Take this road all the way to Coed y Garreg.

Maen Madoc

You will see on your left a standing stone known as Maen Madoc. This is one of the few standing stones with a history in as far as it bears a Latin inscription:

DERVAC I FILIVUS IVSTï(H)IC IACIT which means
(THE STONE) OF DERVACUS, SON OF JUSTUS. HE LIES HERE.

This is not exactly true since the stone was moved from its original position in 1940 from a position some 25 paces to the west of its present location. Prior to 1940 it stood directly beside Sarn Helen which is a Roman road. Sadly we do not know who Dervacus was or why he should have been accorded a 9 ft (2.7m) high monument. But spare him a thought as you pass by.

Maen Madoc on the side of Sarn Helen

At Coed y Garreg cross the Nedd Fechan river and continue upward until at the top of the rise you will reach a waymarked junction. Take the footpath which leads in a north westerly direction and is signposted to Penwyllt. Continue along the broad track until you see another signpost on your left directing you to Penwyllt. The track now becomes a narrow moorland path. Very soon you will come to the substantial ruins of an old farmhouse and its outbuildings. This house, named Pant Mawr, was occupied until the early 1940s when it was demolished by friendly fire! The area was used as a firing range during the Second World War.

Pant Mawr

You are now traversing a fine heather moorland known as Pant Mawr. You have left behind the old red sandstone upland and you are crossing a plateau of limestone and millstone grit pitted by many shake holes. The land is owned by the Cnewr Estate and has been the only upland area in the Brecon Beacons National Park where there has not been free access to roam and enjoy the hills. The path you are on is the only legal definitive footpath crossing the estate. However, the nature of access to this land is being altered by a combination of the Countryside and Rights of Way Act and the estate's participation in Tir Gofal, the Welsh agri-environment scheme.

The footpath across the moor from Pant Mawr farm is easy to follow. The views of the hills to the north and west (Fan Nedd, Fan Fraith, Fan Gyhirych, Fan Hir and Bannau Brycheiniog) form a spectacular changing panorama as you progress.

Rabbit farming

Between 1827 and 1860 this moor was used for the breeding of rabbits for their fur and for the table. The Ordnance Survey map shows a large number of features associated with this land use. A total of 1715 acres (694 hectares) were enclosed for rabbit rearing. At least 80 artificial warrens (pillow mounds) were constructed and within the greater enclosure a variety of other enclosures were built. The most intriguing of these are the small circular dry stone walled pits used as rabbit traps. These lay within small rectangular enclosures that may have been breeding pens. There are five ungated, walled fields used for growing root crops as a supplementary feed.

This rabbit farm was one of three such farms on Fforest Fawr and is by far the largest. The other two, where there is no public access, are on Cefn Cul and south west of Cray reservoir.

Towards the western end of the moor you enter an enclosed area which is part of the Ogof-Ffynnon-Ddu National Nature Reserve.

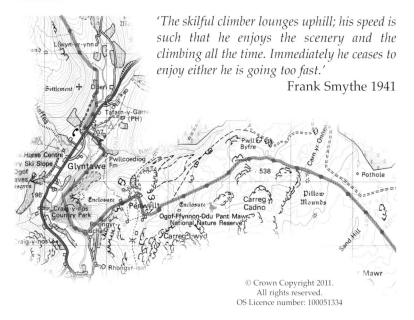

'The skilful climber lounges uphill; his speed is such that he enjoys the scenery and the climbing all the time. Immediately he ceases to enjoy either he is going too fast.'

Frank Smythe 1941

© Crown Copyright 2011.
All rights reserved.
OS Licence number: 100051334

Caves and pavements

Ogof-Ffynnon-Ddu (Cave of the black spring) National Nature Reserve was designated to protect the surface geology, limestone flora and the caves beneath. For many years the South Wales Caving Club has had its headquarters at the old quarry village of Penwyllt. They have extensively explored and mapped the caves of the area. The caves of this National Nature Reserve are managed by the Countryside Council for Wales who own the site in partnership with the South Wales Caving Club.

Limestone pavement in the Ogof Ffynnon Ddu Nature Reserve

65

Within the larger enclosed area of the reserve is yet another enclosure that you are free to enter. This has been created to reduce the grazing pressure on the limestone pavement and to allow for the better development of the plant communities that exist here. Amongst the more interesting plants found are mountain everlasting, autumn gentian and mossy saxifrage. Thirty nine species of birds and 14 species of butterfly have been recorded here. The caves provide a home for rare invertebrates and moths.

As the path descends from the moor the long terrace of quarrymen's cottages that now house the Caving Club comes into view. Head for the right hand end of the terrace and you will connect up with a rough road that will take you to the road leading up to the quarry. When you reach a metalled road to the quarry turn left. Continue on the road until, having passed a bungalow on the right, you see a 'beware of falling rock' sign on the left and a bridle-gate on the right. Go through the bridlegate and follow the path down to a road. On reaching the road turn right, and when you reach Rhonyr Uchaf farm take the bridleway to the left of the house in front of you. Continue along the bridleway until the bridleway divides. Turn sharp left into Craig-y-nos Country Park, owned and run by the Brecon Beacons National Park Authority, and sharp left again to follow the river on your right and make your way over a bridge to the car park and toilets to finish the day.

Craig-y-nos Castle was once the home of Adelina Patti, a famous opera singer

DAY SIX
Mynydd Du:
Craig-y-nos to Llyn y Fan Fawr and Llanddeusant

Distance: 10.5 miles / 16.8 km
Ascent: 2,558 feet / 780 metres   Map: OS Explorer 12

The first day of our excursion into Mynydd Du begins next to Craig-y-nos Castle made famous by its legendary owner Dame Adelina Patti, the great diva, who lived there from 1878 to 1919.

Retrace your steps to the entrance to the Country Park on the bridleway used the previous day where the walk starts. (If the Country Park is closed continue northwards along the road to Tafarn-y-Garreg public house). Go through the car park and head for the Tawe Bridge by leaving the car park at its bottom left hand corner then turn right and right again. As you cross the bridge you will see on your left Nant-Llynfell joining the Tawe immediately above the bridge.

The Llynfell issues out of the Dan-yr-Ogof cave system on the western flank of Glyntawe. Dan-yr-Ogof (a Site of Special Scientific Interest), is the National Show Caves Centre of Wales. Past generations thought that the name of this stream should be Nant-y-Llyn-Pell (The Stream from the Far Lake) believing that its source was at Llyn y Fan Fawr. These days we know better.

Continue upstream with the Tawe on your left until you reach the boundary of Craig-y-nos Country Park.

You might care to cross the bridge (a short detour) to see, on the far bank of the Nant Llynfell, an old flour mill.

This mill is 'Melin-y-Blaenau' (The Blaenau Mill). It used to be called 'Melin-Caeth' (Lord's Mill). It was one of seven such mills in Wales. Farmers from a large area around were compelled to take their corn there for grinding.

After this short detour recross the footbridge to the boundary of Craig-y-nos Country Park.

The next stage of the route is in a northeasterly direction along the old Roman auxiliary road.

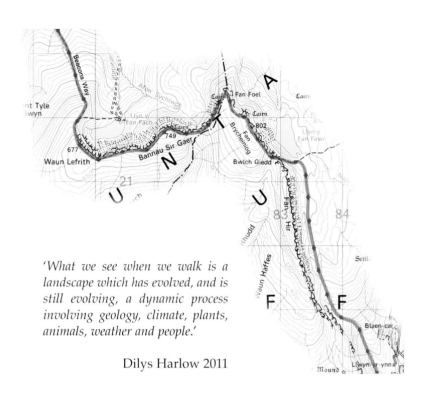

'What we see when we walk is a landscape which has evolved, and is still evolving, a dynamic process involving geology, climate, plants, animals, weather and people.'

Dilys Harlow 2011

© Crown Copyright 2011.
All rights reserved.
OS Licence number: 100051334

Eglwys Caradog

Immediately above you are the crags of Craig-y-Rhiwarth. Near its summit there is a cave named 'Eglwys Caradog'(Caradog's Church). Nobody knows how it came to have this name. There is an elaborate legend linking it with the Roman Emperor Claudius, Caradog's daughter Claudia and St Paul's visit to South Wales with Claudia. St Paul's footprint is said to exist on Cribarth, the hill just west of Craig-y-nos.

Alternatively, you might choose to believe that it should really be Eglwys Cadog, a fifth Century Celtic saint noted for his learning. On the other hand, it could also refer to a monk named Caradog who hid in the cave when he was in flight from his enemy Arglwydd Rhys of Deheubarth. The hills in this part of Wales are alive with legend.

After approximately 700 metres take a path on the left, with a kissing gate and then follow the waymarked path that passes a very large sink hole with a cave entrance and comes out by another kissing gate onto a road in the little hamlet of Callwen.

Having reached the hamlet of Callwen take the path through the kissing gate on the right. Continue along the path through the field to Callwen church. The present church is not the original one and may not be on the original foundations.

The path goes through the churchyard and near the entrance to the church there is a plaque commemorating the victims of an Anson aircraft that crashed on Fan Brycheiniog in December 1939.

Exit the churchyard on to the A4067 road and turn right. Continue along the road to the Tafarn-y-Garreg public house. This was a drovers' inn and was also used by limestone carters on their way to central Brecknock.

At Tafarn-y-Garreg cross the road and take the track opposite which crosses the Tawe by a fine wooden bridge. Will Cefn-Cul, the old shepherd who used to live at the farm across the river said that the bridge was built for his sheep and not for him.

You are about to leave Glyntawe and enter an area called Y Mynydd Du, the Black Mountain. It is an area where (Cymraeg) Welsh is the prominent language and an area where the Normans had to fight hard to establish their ascendancy.

Having crossed the bridge turn right and continue along the riverbank until reaching the gate at SN849173. Here a green lane to your left leads you onto the mountain at a sheep pen. Having reached the open hill turn right and continue along the base of the hill in the direction of the escarpment (Note: the walking can get a bit rough until you get to the end of the enclosed land to your right). When you come to the end of the enclosed land and when you are well and truly out on the hill you will see a track leading towards a stream called the Nant Tawe Fechan. Follow this track and when you reach the stream, at some waterfalls, (marked on the map) you will find a pleasant spot to take a break. It is usually possible to cross the stream at these falls. Do so and follow the stream up on its right bank. This is suggested because there is easier walking underfoot and the view of the stream is better from the right bank. If the stream is in spate proceed up on its west bank.

To your left, towering above, is the escarpment of Fan Hir (Long Peak). At the foot of Fan Hir there is a curious ridge which has been variously interpreted but is now believed to have been formed by a small glacier. This ridge is 0.75miles (1.2km) long. The full escarpment stretches for approx 4.3 miles (7km) as far as Llyn y Fan Fach.

Follow the stream upwards and as it curves closer towards the foot of the escarpment you will see the long morainic ridge. When you reach it climb to its crest and follow its undulations along the foot of the cliffs.

The route follows a stream below the escarpment of Fan Hir

Geologists believe that at the southern end of the ridge there would have been a morainic dam causing a substantial lake to form between the cliffs of the escarpment and the morainic ridge. This was breached a long while ago but were it still to exist it would provide an interesting addition to the landscape.

Continue along the base of the escarpment until when you are wondering 'How much further is this lake?' it will come into view as you crest a small hill. Llyn y Fan Fawr (Lake of the Big Hill) is a moraine-dammed lake with a tendency to freeze over during the winter.

Llyn y Fan Fawr, with its broad and distant views, is an obvious place to take a break.

The water in the lake is crystal clear but unable to sustain fish. It is a home for leeches which are often visible so bathing is not recommended!

Llyn y Fan Fawr (Lake of the Big Hill)

View from summit of Bannau Brycheiniog

At the southwest corner of the lake a well-defined, much used path climbs to the escarpment. When you reach the top, at Bwlch Giedd, turn right and follow a path that leads you all the way round until it descends to Llyn y Fan Fach.

There is a short but steep climb out of Bwlch Giedd to the summit of Fan Brycheiniog which at 2690 feet (820 m) is the highest point in the west of the Brecon Beacons National Park. The views from Fan Brycheiniog are quite spectacular with Llyn y Fan Fawr nestling at the foot of the escarpment. Eastwards you can see Corn Du and Pen y Fan and to the northeast Y Mynyddoedd Duon (The Black Mountains). On a clear day to the south you can see from Somerset to north Cornwall and possibly Lundy Island.

Spend time taking in the view from Fan Brycheiniog then cross the summit plateau to Fan Foel. From here descend, with care in poor visibility, down to Bwlch Blaen-Twrch and Nentydd Blaen-Twrch (SN 816218) where the River Twrch has its source.

The meaning of 'Twrch' is Wild Boar which will remind Welsh speakers of the story in the Mabinogion about Olwen and Culhwch and the Great Wild Boar hunt.

The Great Wild Boar Hunt

Culhwch wished to marry Olwen but, as is often the case in legend, her father was unwilling. However, her father was prepared to give consent providing the young man carried out a series of impossible tasks. The final task was to capture Twrch Trwyth, a formidable wild boar. And so the chase was on! The young man pursued the wild boar with its seven piglets uphill and down dale through Pembrokeshire and Carmarthenshire to the Vale of Loughor and the Amman valley and from there into the Black Mountain. By the time the hunt reached the River Twrch most of the piglets had been slain. Then the wild boar evaded capture by making its way down to the Bristol Channel and swimming across the sea to Cornwall. Here, with the aid of King Arthur and the Knights of the Round Table, the boar met its doom and our hero got his girl.

The curious purpose of all this dashing about was to capture from the wild boar the razor, comb and shears that it kept between its ears so that Olwen's father could be certain of a good shave. Now that really does beggar belief!

There is a steep climb out of Bwlch Blaen-Twrch to Picws Du and the summit of Bannau Sir Gaer 2457 ft (749m). Below lies Llyn y Fan Fach.

Bannau Sir Gaer (2457 feet, 749 metres)

Llyn y Fan Fach, famous for its legend of 'The Lady of the Lake'

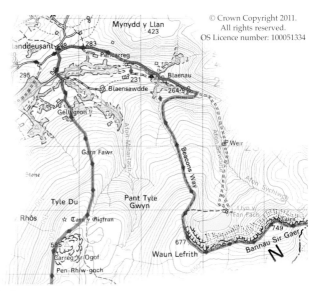

© Crown Copyright 2011.
All rights reserved.
OS Licence number: 100051334

Llyn y Fan Fach
The Legend of the Lady of the Lake

Towards the end of the twelfth century there lived at Blaensawdde, near Llanddeusant, a widow whose husband had died in the struggles of the princes of South Wales against the Normans. One day the widow's son, whilst tending his mother's cattle and other livestock at Llyn y Fan Fach, was astonished to see a beautiful girl sitting on the surface of the water combing her hair using the surface of the water as a mirror. Wishing to become better acquainted he offered her some of his bread and cheese. No doubt aware that there is no such thing as a free lunch she declined his offer saying:

"Cras dy fara"	*"Your bread's hard baked"*
"Nid hawdd fy nala"	*"You don't catch me that easy"*

Then to his great disappointment she sank back into the depths of the lake. When he got home he told his mother what had happened and she advised him to take some unbaked dough the next time.

Next day, before dawn, he went back to the lake hoping to see the girl again. He had to wait for a very long time until the girl reappeared. He held out his hand proffering her some unbaked bread and proclaimed his love. She refused both saying:

"Llaith dy fara"	*"Your bread's unbaked"*
"Ti ni fynna"	*"I will not have you"*

Then with a smile she returned to the depths.

74

He sat down by the lake and wept, much wounded by her rejection. When his mother heard the sad tale she suggested that next time he should take some half-baked bread.

Next morning he ran to the lake and waited for the reappearance of the girl. He waited all day and as night began to fall the most amazing thing happened. He saw cattle walking on the surface of the lake with the girl following behind them. She came towards him and as she stepped upon the shore she allowed the young man to take her hand. She took his bread and promised to be his wife on one condition. If, during their marriage, he were to strike her three times for no good reason she would return to the lake forever. With that she disappeared into the lake.

Almost immediately two beautiful girls arose from the lake accompanied by a tall, elderly, white haired gentleman. The old gentleman spoke to the young man. He said that he could have the girl as his wife providing he could recognise which of the two identical girls who stood before him was the one he had fallen in love with. In truth, they were so much alike that the young man was in a state of despair. Then one of the girls moved her foot slightly forward. It was her that he chose and he had chosen correctly.

The old man said that her dowry would be as many sheep, cattle, goats and horses that she could count in one breath. Then he reminded the young man should he strike his wife on three separate occasions, for no good reason, she would return to the lake forever taking all the animals with her. The Lady of the Lake counted as fast as she could and the animals came out of the lake as fast as she counted. The couple lived happily for many years in the farm called Esgair-llaethdy, a mile from Myddfai, which is there to this day and still inhabited. She bore her husband three sons.

It happened that they were invited to a christening in the district. She complained to her husband that the journey was too far to walk. He told her to get the horse from the field whilst he went into the house to fetch her gloves. On returning he noticed that she had not collected the horse and he lightly tapped her on the shoulder with the gloves saying 'Come, come!' She reminded him of his wedding vows for he had now struck her for the first time.

Some time later when they were guests at a wedding she started crying. Her husband tapped her on her shoulder and asked why she was crying. She replied saying that she was sad because the trials and tribulations of the young couple would soon be starting. Then she reminded him that his troubles would soon be starting unless he was more careful. He had struck her for the second time!

Years passed and the sons grew to be healthy and wise. Then, whilst at a funeral, the wife suddenly started laughing. Her husband touched her on the shoulder and asked her to be quiet. 'When people die then they are out of their misery' she said 'and you have struck the final blow!' She left the funeral and returning home called all the animals by their names, to follow her. She bade her husband farewell and walked towards the lake calling in the animals all the time.

Four oxen ploughing the field responded to her call. They followed her across the mountain still drawing the plough and cut such a deep furrow that it is to be seen to this day.

For many years her sons searched for their mother by the lakeside. Then one day many years later she appeared before the eldest son Rhiwallon and granted him the gift of healing the sick. He became physician to Rhys Gryg, Prince of Dinefwr, and his sons followed after him. It is believed that their skills and knowledge formed the foundation for the work of the Physicians of Myddfai. But that is another story!

Proceed along the top of the cliffs passing the sandstone crags of Cwar-du-Mawr and Cwar-du-Bach. To the west, the millstone grit outcrop of Garreg Las and the limestone outcrop of Carreg yr Ogof come into view across the valley of Twrch Fechan.

Follow the track around the top of the escarpment and start to lose height, taking the track that heads in a northerly direction across Carnau Llwydion. It is shown on the map as a faint pecked line. Proceed along this path across open land before making a steep descent at SN 793237 to a fence line and on down to a wooden gate.

In foggy weather you are advised to take the very well defined track that descends to Llyn y Fan Fach and connects with the Water Board track that leads directly down to a tarmac lane which then ascends to the youth hostel.

Go through the wooden gate and find your way down the rough surface that is crossed and recrossed by a stream. After a time the track swings left and the surface becomes rough pasture. This brings you to a gate onto a tarmac lane. Turn left along the tarmac lane which leads to Gorsddu Farm. As you enter the farm turn sharp right and immediately right again over a stile. Cross the stream and you will soon see the wooden bridge that you must walk over.

Once across the bridge go straight ahead towards the fence. On reaching the fence turn left and take the track that rises following the fence line that is now on your right. This leads to a ruined barn. Take the track that turns right around the barn and having got to the end of the ruin you will see on your left a sunken lane rising steeply to a gate. Take this sunken lane. Go through the gate and climb up the steep bank to the road. On reaching the road turn left and continue for about 0.75 miles (1.2km) to reach the youthhostel.

Llanddeusant Youth Hostel was once a pub called the 'Red Lion'

DAY SEVEN

Llanddeusant Youth Hostel to Carreg Cennen Castle

Distance: 13.6 miles / 21.85 km
Ascent: 2,591 feet / 790m   Map: OS Explorer 12

THE second day of our journey across the Black Mountain takes us through one of the least walked parts of the National Park and requires good map reading ability for the section from Llanddeusant to Carreg Cennen Castle. To aid navigation grid references are frequently used in the text.

Leave the youth hostel and head due south down the metalled lane to the Sawdde Bridge. From this bridge, you begin the longest 1.9 miles (3km) and the greatest ascent 1245ft (380m) of the day.

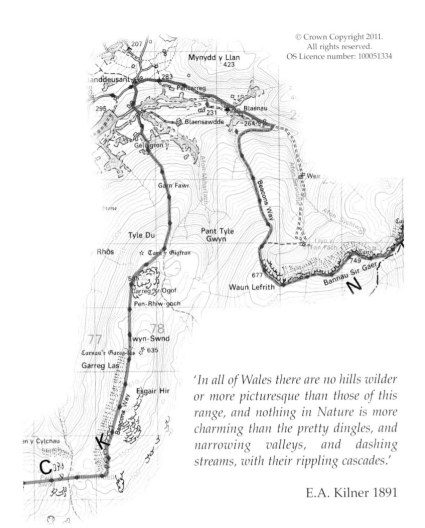

© Crown Copyright 2011.
All rights reserved.
OS Licence number: 100051334

'In all of Wales there are no hills wilder or more picturesque than those of this range, and nothing in Nature is more charming than the pretty dingles, and narrowing valleys, and dashing streams, with their rippling cascades.'

E.A. Kilner 1891

To Carreg Yr Ogof

Cross the bridge and continue up the road (ignoring the signed footpath on the left to Blaensawdde Farm). There is a sign on the right hand side of the road that says Gellygron Farm. On cresting the hill, just before Gellygron Farm, you leave the metalled road and take the bridleway that leads up to the mountain fence. This bridleway is rough under foot, very stony and in wet weather it is somewhat slippery underfoot. It is not very comfortable to the walker.

During the Industrial Revolution this ancient way saw many funeral processions from Ystradgynlais to Llanddeusant. They were the funerals of Llanddeusant men who had crossed the mountain to live and work in the coalfields in and around Ystradgynlais. It was often their wish to be buried back in Llanddeusant. A messenger would be sent over the mountain to arrange the date and time of the funeral where the coffined body was conveyed to Aberdeudwrch, in the heart of the Black Mountain, where the people of Llanddeusant were waiting to receive the body of one of their sons on its final journey home.

You will follow in their footsteps as far as Carreg Yr Ogof.

Part way up the hill the worn track veers to the right. Make certain you continue straight on upwards. The line of the bridleway is signed. Eventually you will reach a gate and a stile that leads onto the open hill. When you cross the stile the exact line of the path ahead is not immediately obvious, but within 100 metres a definite track on the ground can be seen. The route is slightly confused by the existence of other tracks but the line you should take veers to the left and takes you up and over the eastern flank of Tyle Du. As the track rises the limestone crags and quarries of Carreg Yr Ogof come into view.

Carreg Yr Ogof is a carboniferous limestone outcrop and as the name implies there is a cave in its vicinity. You can see the ruins of a number of limekilns.

The track drops down a little and fords the head of the Nant yr Ysgwydd stream. Having crossed the stream leave the bridleway track and veer right along a narrow sheep track to begin the ascent of Carreg Yr Ogof.

There is no one clearly defined track to the summit but the greensward is good to walk on and the limestone crags are easy to surmount. Once on the summit plateau go to its western side and locate the triangulation pillar (SN 777214). This can be difficult to locate in reduced visibility, as it is surrounded by outcropping and quarryworkings.

This location on a clear day reveals the three summits you must cross in order to reach the Brynamman road. Due south lies Garreg Las (SN 777203). Two large Bronze Age cairns, one of which is visible from Carreg Yr Ogof, surmount its northern peak.

North of Carreg yr Ogof, in the direction of Twynllanan, there is a cottage called Beili Glas. It was the childhood home of the writer Richard Vaughan, author of 'Moulded in Earth' and 'Son of Justin'. Both books describe life in the area in the 19th century. He wrote many other books but it was 'Moulded in Earth' and 'Son of Justin' that made him famous in his lifetime when they were turned into a successful television series. They add a layer of meaning to the understanding of this remote area.

Crossing the limestone summit of Carreg yr Ogof

To Carreg Las

From Carreg Yr Ogof head due south and aim for the prominent cairn on the summit of Garreg Las. There is a deep valley between you and Garreg Las which is not obvious from the map. If you veer right you can go round the head of the valley and avoid losing much height. There are several minor tracks leading to Garreg Las. You are certain to connect up with one to make your progress easier.

If you are attempting this section of the route in mist or fog it is essential that you locate the two cairns. If you have trouble retrace your steps and try another day.

When you reach the summit go round to the left of the cairns and having passed the second wheel round to the right, cross two short areas of angular millstone grit rocks and connect with the track that runs just west of south along the western edge of the summit ridge.

This linear track is at times not very distinct but locating it makes all the difference between a comfortable traverse of the ridge and an ankle bending stumble.

The ridge is characterised by a very rough terrain of millstone grit rocks and boulders. There are deep gullies resembling miniature canyons. Only the western edge offers a reasonable passage.

Beware in wet or damp conditions. These rocks can be slippery and should be crossed with caution.

East of Garreg Las, among the tumble of rocks below the summit, there are two partially completed millstone wheels (SN 779203). These wheels probably date from the period of the Napoleonic Wars when the supply of millstone from Brittany ceased due to the war. Certainly, they were made not later than 1830.

You will be walking along the western edge of the ridge for about 1.25 miles (2km). Eventually the rocky surface becomes grassy as the track descends.

To Foel Fraith

A clear track leads from the western edge of Carreg Las (SN 771184) and crosses in a general westerly direction towards Foel Fraith (SN 756183). As you walk down Garreg Las, in the area marked on the map as Godre' Garreg Las, look out for this track across to Foel Fraith because it will indicate where you should come off Garreg Las. The chief consideration in coming off Garreg Las is to avoid crossing too wide an expanse of millstone grit rocks and boulders.

The ascent from the col between Garreg Las and Foel Fraith is only 335 ft (102 m). However, it is one of those hills with many false summits and when you get to the top there is no one obvious high point. Instead it is an area of sink holes and bogs. The summit plateau is very uneven and it seems some time before you reach a point where you actually start to descend on the other side. In fact, it may not be until you start to descend that your next destination, Garreg Lwyd, becomes visible.

To Garreg Lwyd

There is an obvious col to be crossed to reach Garreg Lwyd. You cannot miss it. There is also a good track leading across the col and continuing up the hill to the summit where you will find a large cairn and a triangulation pillar (SN740179) to confirm that you are at the summit. The path to the summit is beautifully graded and you barely notice the ascent. This is particularly surprising because it looked very steep from Foel Fraith. The descent off Garreg Lwyd presents some problem. The summit is a broad flat plateau and it is not possible to discern the next destination and therefore the direction of travel. There is a further problem. If the descent is not well planned you will have to negotiate hazardous rocks and boulders.

At the trig point set the compass on a northwest bearing. Proceed along that line and as you begin to lose height your next destination will come into view. You are aiming for a car park at SN 733188. This will not be obvious at first but a small quarry on the western side of the road will indicate its location. However, you should not head directly for it but contour around the hill until you have passed the areas with rocks and boulders. When you have done this begin the descent across short cropped grassland down to the road and the car park at Pen Rhiw-wen.

George Borrow walked over Pen Rhiw-wen from Llangadog in 1854. This is George Borrow's description of Pen Rhiw-wen taken from his book 'Wild Wales'. (For 'chalk' read 'limestone')

'After the turn I had a huge chalk cliff towering over me on the right and a chalk precipice on my left. Night was now coming on fast and rather to my uneasiness masses of mist began to pour down the sides of the mountain. I hurried on, the road making frequent turnings. Presently the mist swept down upon me and was so thick that I could only see a few yards before me. I was now obliged to slacken my pace and to advance with some degree of caution. I moved on in this way for some time when suddenly I heard a noise, as if a number of carts were coming rapidly down the hill. I stopped and stood with my back close against the high bank. The noise drew nearer and in a minute I saw, indistinctly through the mist, horses, carts and forms of men passing. In one or two cases the wheels appeared to be within a few inches of my feet. At length I gained the top where the road turned and led down a steep descent towards the southwest. It was now quite night and the mist was of the thickest kind. I could just see that there was a frightful precipice on my left so I kept to the right, hugging the side of the hill. As I descended I heard, every now and then, loud noises in the vale probably proceeding from the stone quarries. When I had proceeded about a mile I saw blazes down below resembling those of furnaces'.

(The blazes he described were from the ironworks at Cwter Fawr which is now known as Brynamman).

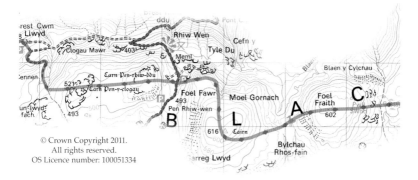

© Crown Copyright 2011.
All rights reserved.
OS Licence number: 100051334

Cross the road at Foel Fawr and to the left of the old quarry. Once at the top bear left and cross the moor the short distance to the top of the hill (Pen Rhiw-ddu) with its large Bronze Age cairn. Continue west to Carn Pen-y-clogau (SN 717186) where there are views to the south across the Aman Valley with Dyffryn Tywi (the Vale of Tywi) to the north.

Immediately south of Carn Pen-y-clogau is an area called Banc y Cerrig-pwdron – (Bank of rottenstone). This was one of many areas across the limestone outcrops on Mynydd Du where rottenstone was extracted a century or two back. Rottenstone is weathered impure shale of limestone. It was ground into a powder and used for polishing and burnishing tin plate and copper manufactured in the lower Tawe Valley near Swansea. It was also exported to the Midlands. Rottenstone deposits extended eastwards across the limestone country of the Black Mountain as far as Cribarth above Craig-y-nos.

Girls from Cwmllynfell and Cwmtwrch would make the five mile round trip to Pen yr Helyg three times daily, weather permitting, transporting the stone by panniered ponies. The girls received one shilling per journey. This stone, prior to the days of Brasso, was also used as a household metal polish.

Descend from Carn Pen-y-clogau in a westerly direction until you reach the bridleway at (SN 711186). This track was once the turnpike road from Brynamman to Llangadog. Follow this old turnpike road in a northerly direction until reaching the tarmac road at Brest Cwm Llwyd.
On the southern side of this road are the grass covered remains of some early limekilns (SN 706193). Keep on this road for a short

distance until reaching the bend at SN 704193. Take the path on your left and head for Banc Wernwgan. When the path becomes less distinct, head for the base of Pentir Blaencennen. When you can see the head of a deep valley, walk towards it to make sure you pass just above. Once past the gulley a path becomes clear that proceeds in a westerly direction. You eventually cxome to the remains of an enclosure and a road (SN 685186).

Prior to reaching Pâl y Cwrt there is an old ruin, formerly a cultivated holding called Bryniau, close to old lime workings. The word pâl comes from the French word pâle meaning enclosure. Cwrt means court hence the 'Enclosure of the Court'. It may be that Pâl y Cwrt had been associated with Carreg Cennen Castle.

At SN 675183 there are earth mounds, called Beddau'r Derwyddon. They are not the graves of the Druids as the name implies but pillow mound, which are medieval warrens for the breeding of rabbits both for the table and their fur.

Turn left and continue along the road until you arrive at the entrance to Brondai Farm (SN673180) on your right. After a stile by a farm gate the track passes to the left behind farm buildings before turning left between fields. Follow a grassy path, fenced on both sides, (heading N) which is on the left of another farm track. The path swings right and crosses the farm track and can be very muddy as it climbs the hill. Here you will have fine views of the castle on your left. The woodland below the castle cliffs is a Site of Special Scientific Interest and is owned and managed by the National Park Authority.

At the end of this enclosed path go over a stile by a metal gate and head down the hill in a NE direction. At a path junction bear left following the castle logo on the fingerpost. Towards the bottom of the hill the path veers sharp left and crosses a farm track. Here you will see a stile with 'Castle avoiding farmyard' displayed. Cross the stile (heading N) and descend along a wet path to a wooden footbridge across the stream.

After another stile you cross a more substantial wooden bridge. This was erected for the National Park Authority by Cardiff University Officer Training Corps. As you cross the bridge you can see where willow logs have been driven into the riverbed to try and stop water eroding the bank.

Cross the bridge turn right and then sharp left following the castle logo signs up a steep grassy track which takes you through the woodland owned by the National Park Authority to Carreg Cennen Castle.

At the top of the hill the castle is well worth a visit and is open from 9.30am to 8.00pm. Keeping the castle on your left a tarmac path descends to a café/shop and then bears left to the car park.

There is an excellent café and shop in the old barn providing good Welsh fare. Bernard Llewellyn, the owner of the farm and castle has a herd of old long horned cattle as well as rare breeds of sheep.

Carreg Cennen Castle

The Castle

Carreg Cennen Castle was the ancient centre and stronghold of the Commote of Is-Cennen which lay to the south of the River Tywi and south east of the township of Llandeilo. This site was a stronghold long before the Norman lords recognised its strategic importance. The earliest documentary evidence for a castle on this site dates from 1248 and the existing castle belongs to the late 13th or early 14th Century. It was deliberately dismantled shortly after the Wars of the Roses (in the 15th Century) because it was thought too much of a threat to the monarchy. Finds of coins on the hill dating from the 1st and 4th century suggest that the site was occupied during the Roman occupation.

The castle stands on an outlier of carboniferous limestone set amongst the Old Red Sandstone. The limestone crag is a zone of folding and thrusting known as the Carreg Cennen Disturbance and is a geological Site of Special Scientific Interest. The woodland between the castle and the river is a nature reserve.

Carreg Cennen Castle is perched on the top of a 100 metre limestone crag

DAY 8
Carreg Cennen to Bethlehem

> Distance: 6.8 miles 10.9km
> Ascent: 787 feet 240 metres   Map: OS Explorer 12

Having made sure you visit the castle take the road leading north-westerly to Castle View Farm (SN 661196). From there take the north-easterly path to Cilmaenllwyd Farm (SN 665199). Pass through the farm and keep on a north-easterly heading hand railing a fence on your left. At a small stream cross a stile and ford the stream and then head north across a field and cross an old fence line again hand railing a fence on your left. After another stile an obvious path heads north-easterly by the side of a stone wall before passing some old quarry workings. Follow the path to a ladder stile at SN 667209 and then cross a rough field (heading NNE and following waymarking posts) to arrive at a stile by a tarmac road at the corner of Helgwm forest. Turn right at the road and continue along it until reaching the crossroads at SN 679218.

At the crossroads take the footpath straight ahead that goes in a north-easterly direction (north of Carn Powell) into the forest plantation at Carreglwyd (SN 687225). Continue heading NW on a descending track through the plantation and on reaching the fence on its far side turn sharp right and take the easterly track that rises steeply to Bwlch y Gors. Shortly after leaving the plantation bear left along a raised embankment by the side of a new fence to cross a small stream. As you ascend, at Bwlch y Gors, there are two tracks. One goes straight ahead in a north-easterly direction below Trichrug. The other which you will take, bears left through a gate and leads down towards Garn Goch. (This is an unclassified county road).

From Bwlch y Gors follow the old grass track down to Garn-wen Farm (SN 695239) which lies south-east of the Iron Age fort of Carn Goch. Just beyond the farm you arrive at the common.
Follow the road to the lane leading to Tan-y-lan (SN 696242) on your right where you will see an obvious path on your left leading to the north-eastern entrance into this 300 BC fort. This fort is among the largest, if not the largest, Iron Age fort in Wales. It is 2296 ft (700m) long by 656 ft (200m) wide.

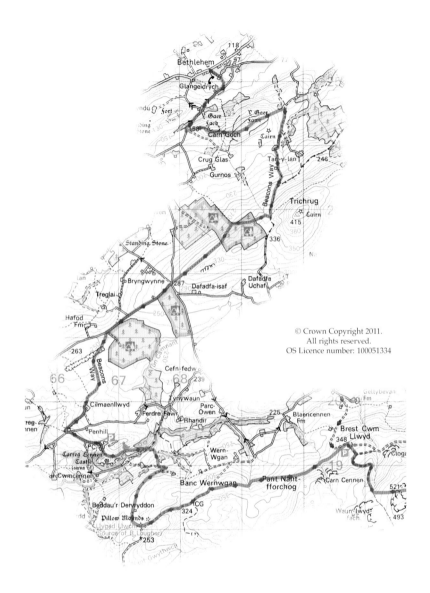

© Crown Copyright 2011.
All rights reserved.
OS Licence number: 100051334

'The early Iron Age hill fort of Garn Goch, or the Red Mount, is so called because of the bronze-coloured bracken which distinguishes it in the autumn and perhaps also because of the Old Red Sandstone hill on which it stands.'

Edmund Mason 1975

Garn Goch Iron Age Fort

There are two fine hillforts on the same hill both of similar construction and both of the same date. A small gap divides the lower fort (Y Gaer fach) from the main summit where the larger camp (Y Gaer fawr) sits.

Garn Goch Iron Age Fort

The larger fort is surrounded by a massive collapsed stone rampart which originally would have been 16 ft (5m) thick. There is an outer wall on the south-east side which may be the remains of an earlier fort. In the main wall it is possible to discern the remnants of at least six entrances which would have been roofed over with lintels. There are the remains of a small 'postern gate' on the southern side of the main fort which is well worth a visit. The original large stones are mainly in situ. Many of them fell inwards and were re-erected in Victorian times.

The remains of the north-east entrance suggest it consisted of twin passages 50 ft (14m) apart. Each was 6.5 feet (2m) wide and 32 ft (10m) to 36 ft (11m) long and lined with large upright slabs and roofed. The rampart was thickened for a total length of 98 ft (30m). Little remains of the northern portal but a large fallen slab at the bottom of a crater in the rubble of the rampart.

There is a large stone cairn on a natural sandstone ridge in the interior of the fort. This cairn is 10 ft (3m) high, 188 ft (55m) long and 65 ftt (20m) wide. Although it has the appearance of a Neolithic Long Cairn it is almost certainly a burial cairn of Bronze Age date.

Not far from the cairn, near the middle of the fort, is a marshy area, which as recently as 1906 contained an oval pool 131 ft (40m) by 49 ft (15m). The western side of the rampart rises to 21 ft (6.5m) while the remaining rampart is of a lower height.

Exiting the fort at its north-westerly point (SN 688242) and carefully climbing down, cross the gulley to Y Gaer Fach. Then head in a westerly direction following a path that leads down to an interpretation board for the site. At the lane turn right and after a few metres right again at the T junction downhill towards Bethlehem.

Follow the road until reaching Bethlehem Chapel (SN 687249). Turn left onto the footpath and cross the fields that lead to Banc-y-fedwen. Keep to the left of the house and follow the driveway to the road where you turn right for the village renowned for its Post Office which is now a private house. The quiet little Post Office used to be a place of great activity at Christmas. Christmas Cards posted here used to carry the Bethlehem postmark. This tradition still remains and is carried out in the part-time Post Office in the former village school (now a Community Centre). The normal opening hours are Tuesday 10-12, Thursday 2-4 but as Christmas approaches all that changes. From the 1st to the 21st of December it is open Monday to Friday 10-4 and on Saturdays 10-12 noon.

You have now reached your journey's end.

Total Distance Walked : 94.65 miles (151.7km)

Total Ascent: 18,682 feet (5696m)

GENERAL INFORMATION

The Beacons Way Art Trail
Linked to the Beacons Way is an Art Trail which has been developed by the Brecknock Museum and the Brecon Beacons Park Society. Along the route of each of the eight sections of the Beacons Way may be discovered a block of locally quarried stone into which has been set a relief image created by one of eight artists working in the National Park. Some of these stones are set into banks and others into walls. Together, the images show very diffent responses to the landscape, its ecology and mythology. A record of the images may be obtained by taking rubbings of them with a wax crayon or soft pencil on tracing paper.

Locations of the images
Day One: SO 318235, Day Two: SO 282240, Day Three: SO 205217, Day Four: SO 036205, Day Five: SN 861157, Day Six: SN 798222, Day Seven: SN 670192, Day Eight: SN 683248

Website Information
Further information about The Beacons Way may be found on the Brecon Beacons Park Society website:
                www.breconbeaconsparksociety.org

Reporting Problems
If you have experienced a problem or identfy an improvement required on Access Land or Public Rights of Way within the Brecon Beacons National Park please let the authority know by completing a form which can be found on the Brecon Beacons Park Authority web site.

Tourist Information Centres

Abergavenny
Swan Meadow, Monmouth Road, Abergavenny,
Monmouthshire NP7 5HH.
Tel: 01873 857588
Email: abergavenny@breconbeacons.org
Open: Summer 7 days 10.00am – 5.30pm Winter 7 days 10.00 am
– 4.30 pm.

Brecon
Cattle Market Car Park,
Tel: 1874 622485
Email: brecontic@powys.gov.uk

Hay-on-Wye
The Craft Centre, Oxford Road, (by main car park)
Hay-on-Wye HR3 SD6.
Tel: 01497 820144, E-mail: post@hay-on-wye.co.uk
Open: Easter- October 10.00am - 5.00pm daily
November - Easter 11.00am - 1.00pm and 2.00pm - 4.00pm daily

National Park Visitor Centre and Tea Rooms (Mountain Centre)
Tel: 01874 623366
Email: visitorcentre@brecombeacons.org
Open each day at 9.30am   Close Mar-June 5.00pm   July - Aug
6.00pm
Sept-Oct 5.00pm Nov-Feb 4.30pm
Web: www.breconbeacons.org

Llandeilo
Car Park, Crescent Road, Llandeilo, Carmarthenshire SA19 4EU.
Tel: 01558 824226
E-mail: llandeilotic@carmarthenshire.gov.uk
Open: Summer 6 days 09.00am–4.00pm Winter 2 days week ends
9.00am –5.00pm

Llandovery
The Heritage Centre, Kings Road, Llandovery, Carmarthenshire
SA20 0AW.
Tel: 01550 720693

Email: llandoverytic@breconbeacons.org
Open: Easter - October: 9.30am - 1.30pm and 1.45pm - 5.00pm daily
November - Easter: 10 - 5.00pm
Web: www.breconbeacons.org

Waterfalls Centre
Pontneathvaughan Road, Pontneddfechan, Nr Glyneath SA11 5NR
Tel: 01639 721795
Email: waterfalls.centre@breconbeacons.org
Open: April - November 9.30am - 1.00pm and 1.30pm - 5.00pm, seven days a week. November - April 9.30am - 1.00pm and 1.30pm - 3.00pm weekends only.

Blaenavon World Heritage Centre
Church Street, Blaenavon
Tel: 01495 742333
Open: April - September: Tuesday - Sunday 9.00am - 5.00pm
Bank Holidays and October - March 9.00am - 4.00pm
Closed Christmas Eve to New Years Day

Crickhowell Resource & Information Centre
Beaufort Street, Crickhowell NP8 1BN
Tel: 01873 811970 www.crickhowellinfo.org.uk
Open 7 Days a Week: 10.00am - 5.00pm daily (10.00am -15.00pm Sundays November to February)

Talgarth
The Tower Shop, Talgarth LD3 0BW
Tel: 01874 712226
Open: Easter-October

Brecon Beacons National Park Visitor Services
Visit the web site:
www.breconbeacons.org for information about all aspects of the National Park. Enquiries may be made directly to:
Visitor Services Department, Brecon Beacons National Park Authority, Plas y Ffynnon, Cambrian Way, Brecon, Powys LD3 7HP.
Tel: 01874 624437, E-mail: enquiries@breconbeacons.org
Web: www.breconbeacons.org
Office hours 08.30 -17.00 Monday-Friday.

Public Transport

The Tourist Information Centres will provide up to date information on public transport. However, visitors need to be aware, that as with most rural areas, there is not much of it about. Check it out very carefully.

Sunday travel presents some problems
In recent years the Brecon Beacons National Park Authority has received grant aid to provide an extensive Sunday service during the summer months. The routes taken in and around the Park provide transport links unavailable during the week. The routes and the timetable vary from year to year. It is a very good and useful service and information is available from Tourist Information Centres and from the head office of the National Park Authority and on the website www.visitbreconbeacons.com

Abergavenny
Train Services
North to Hereford, Shrewsbury, Manchester with links to Birmingham etc.
South to Newport and Cardiff for connections to London, the West Country etc.

Bus Services
West to Brecon along A40 calling at Crickhowell, Bwlch, Talybont.
North to Hereford.
South and South-West to Newport & Cardiff. Buses go via Heads of Valleys road as well as Cwmbran.
East to Monmouth.

Brecon
Bus Services
To Abergavenny (see Abergavenny above).
To Hereford via Talgarth and Hay on Wye.
To Llandovery via Sennybridge. At Llandovery connections may be made for Llangadog and the mid Wales railway line.
To Craig-y-nos via Sennybridge and south to Swansea.
To Merthyr Tydfil via Libanus and Storey Arms (and then by bus or train to Cardiff etc).
Limited service to Builth.

Craig-y-nos
Bus Services
To Swansea and Brecon.

Llandovery
Train Services
On Heart of Wales Line
Trains to Swansea via
Llangadog and through to Shrewsbury.

Bus Services
To Brecon via Sennybridge
To Llandeilo where there are connections to Swansea and West Wales.
Limited service to Lampeter.

Llangadog
Train Services
On Heart of Wales Line trains to Llandovery through to Shrewsbury and south to Swansea.

Bus Services
South to Llandeilo where there are bus connections and north to Llandovery where there is a connection to Brecon.

Taxis
The local Information Centres will be able to advise you as will the National Park Travel Guide. This guide is also available at www.visitbreconbeacons.com

Mobile Phones: A warning
Walkers are reminded that because of the mountainous terrain mobile phones do not operate in large areas of the Brecon Beacons National Park. This is particularly important if walkers are planning to contact car drivers or taxis to pick them up at the end of the day. There are public telephone boxes at or near the end of all sections of the Trail.

Weather Forecast
A useful weather forecast for the Brecon Beacons can be found on www.metoffice.com/outdoor/mountainsafety/brecon.html

Accommodation
The Tourist Information Offices, particularly those open throughout the year, are the most useful source of information concerning the range of accommodation available.

The Brecon Beacons Park Society's Website: www.breconbeaconsparksociety.org will also carry information concerning accommodation enroute.

The youth hostels at Llwyn y Celyn below Storey Arms (tel 01874 624261) and Llanddeusant (tel 01550 740218) are very popular and you are advised to book well in advance.

Some Further Reading
These publications listed below were consulted during the writing of this guide.

Brecon Beacons National Park National Park Guide No. 5
Her Majesty's Stationery Office 1978.

Out of print but worth searching for. The most comprehensive guide to the Brecon Beacons National Park:

Brecon Beacons. The Official National Park Guide
Roger Thomas with photographs by Harry Williams.
Pevensey Guides 2002.

The Canals of the Welsh Valleys and their Tramroads
D.D & J.M. Gladwin, The Oakwood Press, 1991.
The Brecknock and Abergavenny Canal and the many tramroads associated with it (although not strictly in 'the valleys') are described and their histories recorded.

Canal – The Brecon & Aergavenny (section of the Monmouthshire & Brecon) Canal by John Norris
A very comprehensive guide to the canal written primarily for canal boat users but of equal interest to walkers.

Carreg Cennen Castle
CADW 1990
The Official Guide

Classic Landforms of the Brecon Beacons
Richard Shakesby, The British Geomorphological Research Group 2002

A 45 page superbly illustrated account of the formation of the landforms in the Black Mountain (Mynydd Du), Fforest Fawr and Central Brecon Beacons.

Hills and Vales of the Black Mountain District
Richard Baker-Gabb
First published 1913. Reprinted by Lapridge Publications. Still available from bookshops. A very informative, interesting and useful account of the Monmouthshire Black Mountains.
Llanthony Priory
O.E.Craster. TD, MA, FSA
Her Majesty's Stationery Office 1963
Department of the Environment Official Handbook

Mynydd Du and Fforest Fawr: The Evolution of an Uplands Landscape in South Wales.
David K. Leighton
Royal Commission on the Ancient and Historical Monuments of Wales. 1997
This account explores the history of human activity in the western upland area of the National Park from the end of the last glaciation to the present.

Powys – The Buildings of Wales
Richard Haslam
Penguin and University of Wales Press. 1979

Prehistoric Peoples – their life and legacy
Peter Dorling and David Brinn, Brecon Beacons National Park 1996

Shadows in a Landscape. Llangynidr. The Evolution of a Community.
Published by Llangynidr Local History Society 2000
An account of the history, life and landscape of a Breconshire village and the countryside around it.

Stone and Steam in the Black Mountains by David Tipper
Blorenge Books 1975 reprint 1994
The classic account of the building of the Grwyne fawr Reservoir in the Monmouthshire Black Mountains.

Guidebooks

In recent years the interest in walking has much increased. Walking magazines are flourishing. National and local Trails have been created and there has never been such a selection of walking guides available. Given this abundance it is difficult to make a choice. Listed below are some of the titles currently available.

Aircraft crash sites and the stories behind them
Brecon Beacons National park Authority

Circular Walks in the Brecon Beacons National Park
Tom Hutton, Gwasg Carreg Gwalch 1998

40 Classic Walks in the Brecon Beacons National Park
Chris Barber, Blorenge books 2010

Walks in the Craig y nos area and Upper Tawe Valley
Brecon Beacons National Park Authority

Walks from Abergavenny
Walks from The Mountain Centre
Brecon Beacons National Park Authority

Many of the walking guidebooks to the Brecon Beacons National Park can be purchased from the Tourist Information Centres in the Brecon Beacons National Park.

> *'The Beacons Way, a major project developed by the Brecon Beacons Park Society, was launched on the 20th May 2005 with much razzmatazz. That was only the beginning and the story continues.'*
>
> John Sansom 2006

A TRIBUTE TO JOHN SANSOM

John Sansom exploring part of the route in 2005

John Sansom, a long standing member of the Brecon Beacons Park Society was the originator and main author of 'The Beacons Way' and his name will always be associated with it. He often said that the best and most fulfilling time of his life was a total commitment to his beloved Black Mountains and Brecon Beacons.

John sadly died in Nevill Hall Hospital, Abergavenny, following a period of ill-health on 24th June 2006. His ashes were scattered in Cwm-gu which was one of John's favourite places on the walk and set into a wall (SO 202219) can be found a stone plaque inscribed with John's name, the dates of his life and the simple statement: 'He created the Beacons Way.' Beneath these words is a carving of the Beacons Way waymark.

Memorial to John Sansom in Cwm-gu

OTHER TITLES PUBLISHED BY BLORENGE BOOKS

Mysterious Wales by Chris Barber
Hando's Gwent (Volume 1) by Chris Barber
40 Classic Walks in the Brecon Beacons National Park by Chris Barber
In Search of Owain Glyndwr by Chris Barber
Eastern Valley – The Story of Torfaen by Chris Barber
Exploring Blaenavon Industrial Landscape World Heritage Site by Chris Barber
The Clydach Gorge by John van Laun
Exploring Kilvert Country by Chris Barber
Llanover Country by Chris Barber
The Legacy of King Arthur by Chris Barber
Arthurian Caerleon by Chris Barber
In the Footsteps of Alexander Cordell by Chris Barber
Collected Poems by Anne Marie Barber
Sacred Springs by Paul Davis
Rape of the Fair Country by Alexander Cordell

Enquiries welcome: Tel: 01873 856114

www.blorenge-books.co.uk